THE GARDENS OF
FLORENCE

THE GARDENS OF
FLORENCE

RIZZOLI
NEW YORK

PHOTOGRAPHS
BY
ALESSANDRO
ALBRIZZI

TEXT
BY
MARY JANE POOL

INTRODUCTION
BY
ILEANA
CHIAPPINI DI SORIO

ACKNOWLEDGMENTS

Many doors and garden gates have been opened to us in the preparation of this book. We are most grateful for the warm welcome we received in Florence, and hope old friends and new friends will feel their time well spent when they have a finished book in hand. The compiling of material has taken three years—a passion for romantic gardens of history has urged us on.

Landscape architect Bruce Kelly has been our very helpful consultant on plant species and historical references.

We were fortunate to be able to photograph the gardens of Sir Harold Acton, Marchese and Marchesa Piero Antinori, Aureliano and Maria Teresa Benedetti, the Budini Gattai family, Mrs. Wanda Ferragamo, Barone Amerigo Franchetti, the family of the Marchesi Frescobaldi, Marchese and Marchesa Lorenzo Ginori Lisci, Marchese Amerigo Gondi, Marchese and Marchesa Bernardo Gondi, Marchese Piero Malenchini, Carlo and Gioia Marchi, the Marchi family, Mrs. Anna Mazzini, Conte Filippo Pandolfini, Marchese and Marchesa Giuseppe Paternò Castello di San Giuliano, Mr. Pier Francesco Scarselli, Marchese Giuseppe Torrigiani di Santa Cristina, the Torrigiani Malaspina di Fosdinovo family, and Mrs. Patricia Volterra.

Permissions and archival material were given to us by the Mayor of the City of Florence, Mr. Giorgio Morales; Mrs. Mila Pieralli, President of the Province of Florence; Arch. Lionello Boccia, Curator of the Museo Stibbert; Mr. Ruggero Pentrella, Director of the Beni Ambientali and Architettonici for the provinces of Florence and Pistoia; Arch. Giorgio Galletti for the Boboli garden; Father Superior Mario Franchi for the Cloister of San Lorenzo; the President of the Foundation of the Villa I Tatti; Father Superior Priore Alberto Simoni for the Convent of San Marco; Mrs. Elvira Pajetta, President of the Institute of the Spedale degli Innocenti; Mrs. Fiorenza Scalia, Director of the Museo di Firenze com'era; Mr. Gerald Ewald, Director of the German Institute; Mr. Francesco Lenzini, Director of the Cassa di Risparmio di Pisa; Mr. Natale Rusconi and Mr. Maurizio Saccani of the Villa San Michele; and Mr. Piero Tacconi, Director of the Ombrellino Trade Center.

We particularly want to thank Contessa Maria Teresa Guicciardini Corsi Salviati and Marchesa Alessandra Torrigiani for their very special efforts on our behalf. And we truly appreciate the kindness of Marchesa Maria Cristina Ginori Lisci, Stefano Bucci, Achille Tempestini of the German Institute, Dolores and Luciano Guarnieri, Contessa Paola Sannazzaro Natta, Arch. Giuseppe Chiggiotti, Alessandra Marchi Pandolfini, and Marchese and Marchesa Andrea Malenchini.

The writings of Sir Harold Acton and the late Marchese Leonardo Ginori Lisci have given us much good information and personal insights that have been most helpful. The research in London by Bettina McNulty has been invaluable.

We are indebted to our publisher, Gianfranco Monacelli, for seeing the merits of such a book, and to our editor, Robert Janjigian, for his thoughtful guidance in its creation.

The gardens in and around Florence have inspired many writers through the centuries. Their impressions have inspired us, and enriched our text. We thank them.

A.A., M.J.P.

First published in the United States of America in 1992 by
Rizzoli International Publications, Inc.
300 Park Avenue South, New York, NY 10010

Library of Congress Cataloging-in-Publication Data

Albrizzi, Alessandro
    The Gardens of Florence / photographs by Alessandro
Albrizzi; text by Mary Jane Pool; introduction by Ileana
Chiappini di Sorio.
        p.   cm
    Includes bibliographical references and index.
    ISBN 0-8478-1488-2
    1. Gardens—Italy—Florence 2. Gardens—Italy—
Florence—Pictorial works I. Pool, Mary Jane. II. Title.
SB466.I82F563 1992   91-32075
712'.0945'51—dc20   CIP

Designed by Mary Jane Pool and Miki Denhof
Map by T. R. Lundquist
Printed and bound by CS Graphics pte ltd, Singapore

Endpapers, page 1: *Angel in the
courtyard grotto at the Palazzo Pitti.*
Pages 2-3: *San Lorenzo cloister.*
Pages 4-5: *Palazzo Pitti.*
Pages 6-7: *Palazzo Antinori.*
Pages 8-9: *Villa Capponi.*
Pages 10-11: *Villa La Gamberaia.*
Frontispiece: *Villa Capponi.*
Page 14: *Palazzo Feroni.*
Page 16: *Palazzo Incontri, now the
German Institute.*

CONTENTS

INTRODUCTION
BY ILEANA CHIAPPINI DI SORIO

The very notion of a garden cannot be separated from its mythical, religious, and artistic components. The earthly paradise and the archaic world, imagined as very beautiful gardens, reflect the harmony achieved between humanity and nature.[1] With the "Biblical and Homeric texts, they [even] became a mental structure of poetry."[2] Starting with Homer, the garden was thought to be imbued with the presence of the gods, thereby taking on a sacred aura. Locating a garden adjacent to a sanctuary was a tradition going back to the Aegean world, with its link to the myth of vegetation.[3] The rapport between gardens and agrarian religiosity became more powerful in the historical era, when the encompassed space included votive symbols, trees, and sacred wellsprings.[4] Moreover, the Dionysian cult, which spread uninterruptedly throughout Italy despite official condemnation, involved the concept of the sacred garden.

However, the idea of the garden as a place for relaxing and getting together did not emerge until the third century A.D., first in Hellenistic Greece, then in southern Italy. It finally reached Rome,[5] most likely as part of the Oriental influences exerted chiefly by Egypt and Mesopotamia.

The Egyptians grew flowers to decorate their houses and temples. Pictorial material unearthed in their tombs points out the function and the organization of the garden as well as the practical details of its use and maintenance. Devised as an additional living space and laid out within the boundaries of the residence, the garden was an area for growing trees and fruit. A major decorative element was a pond, which, along with a canal system, helped to irrigate the soil and to cool the air.[6]

The artistic literature of Mesopotamian civilization provides ample information about gardening, especially botany. Indeed, the plant inventory supplied by Marduk-apal-iddin is a generous roster of what he cultivated in his garden. The presence of large areas of terrain functioning as gardens was likewise indicated by monuments decorated with reliefs; for instance,

Opposite: *Rose trellis and hortus conclusus. Miniature by the Master of King Renato, fifteenth century, Boccaccio, Teselde delle nozze di Emilia, Vienna, National Library.*

1. R. Assunto, *Paessaggio e l'estetica: Concetto di giardino* vol. 3 (Naples: Giannini, 1973), 193, 195—196. Particularly 196—198; G.C. Argan, "Giardino e Parco: Problemi generali," *Enciclopedia universale dell'arte* vol. 6 (Florence: Sansoni, 1956), 154; L. Puppi, "L'ambiente, il paesaggio e il territorio," *Storia dell'arte italiana* (Turin: Einaudi, 1980), 77.
2. G. Venturi, *Le scene dell'Eden: Teatro, arte, giardini nella letteratura italiana,* (Ferrara: Bovolenta, 1979), 104.
3. P. Grimal, "Mondo classico," *Enciclopedia universale dell'arte* vol 6 (Florence: Sansoni, 1958), 162.
4. Argan, "Giardino e Parco: Problemi generali," 156.
5. Grimal, "Mondo classico,"162, 164.
6. S. Bosticco and G. Garlini, "Antichità: Oriente antico," *Enciclopedia universale dell'arte* vol 6 (Florence: Sansoni, 1958), 161—162.

Earthly Paradise. Miniature by the Limbourg brothers, fifteenth century, in Les tres riches heures du duc de Berry, Chantilly, Musée Condé.

the arched architectural insertions in scenographic contexts showed huge, graduated hanging gardens resembling those in Babylon, which were regarded by Antiquity as one of the Seven Wonders of the World. Similarly, the hunting scenes on the bas-reliefs of Assurbanipal certify the existence of parks surrounding the royal palaces of the Iranian emperors. Furthermore, the palace of Ctesiphon in Taq-i-Kisra not only stood inside a park, but offered an architectural conception of the garden; during rigorous winters, the fluorescences of plants were replaced by a large carpet whose decorative "garden" design was studded with precious stones. Under the Arab domination, this garden was lost; but the memory persisted among the Persians, so that even today they maintain the custom of so-called garden carpets.[7]

In the wake of the Persians, the royal parks, also known as "paradises," exerted an influence on the Greeks; and the renown of Cyrus's garden in Sardis was probably a determining factor in the creation of the "royal paradises." The latter were planned in geometric terms according to an established order, which, taking hunting into account, hewed even more closely to Persian tradition.

Sicily, which, given its peculiar geographic position, was under Greek hegemony, became the first Italian island to introduce gardens and "paradises." One example was Gelon's "Horn of Amaltheia" in Syracuse; and there is also information available about a small garden that was designed for Hiero II's ship.[8] It was, no doubt, under the impact of the Sicilian "paradises" and the customs drawn from Greek civilization that Rome began ushering in gardens around the third century A.D. Cicero used words of Greek origin to describe the art of gardening, *ars topiaria*. However, for the Romans, "topiary" did not mean pruning leaves and bushes into artistic shapes. Rather, it was meant to deliberately express nature—representing the country—which could not be divorced from the presence of the deities; this was the goal of the idylls and epigrams of painters and poets. Thus, while the formal terminology was derived from the Greeks, the themes accentuated the Roman taste, which stemmed from the Dionysian repertoire and sacred rituals.

The first Roman gardens may have been laid out in the fields of the military drilling grounds. Cicero recalled the gardens of Scipio Emilianus and Junius Brutus; however, by then, the Roman villas with gardens were already spreading throughout Latium. In the middle of the first century A.D., the "domus Tampiliana" on the Quirinal had, according to Cicero, incorporated an ancient "silva" (forest); and, on the right bank of the Tiber, Caesar set up his Roman park known as the "Horti Caesaris," which was opened for public use after his death. During the Imperial age, the demand for gardens greatly increased, and numerous examples have been recorded with the modern boundaries of Rome's historical center; they included the Pompeian Gardens near Piazza di Spagna, the Lucullan Gardens at Trinità dei Monti, and the nearby Sallustian Gardens on Via Veneto.

The Roman garden assumed geometric forms in harmony with the architecture of the manor house, with which it was united as an

7. H. Goetz, "Oriente antico," *Enciclopedia universale dell'arte* (Florence: Sansoni, 1958).
8. Grimal, "Mondo classico," 162.

integral part. It was subdivided by arbors, colonnades, and fences made of wickerwork. Often, the rustic atmosphere was emphasized by grottoes, brooks, shrines, and statues drawn from mythology and ancient Dionysian iconography; thus, one could see Priapus superimposed on the ancient "fascinus" or satyrs issuing from the ancient tradition of Sylvanus and Faunus.[9]

The walls were decorated with ivy, and also maidenhair fern, as well as various shrubs, while cypresses were planted along the lanes. The Roman writer Plinius the Younger penned charming depictions of several gardens whose positions, especially in their relation to the respective villa and the natural landscape, were studied in advance; while livelier and more direct images have survived in the pictorial documents of that epoch. Finally, an even more precise idea of the garden's form may be gained from the archaeological remnants and from the description of the Villa Adriana (Hadrian's Villa) in Tivoli. Apparently designed by the emperor, and then built between 125 and 135 A.D., this rare and sublime villa allows one to trace all the features making up the elegant and rigorous grandeur of the imperial gardens. The gardens of the Italian Renaissance derive at least partially from those Roman forebears. Likewise in Tivoli, the Villa d'Este was ultimately inspired by its neighbor, the Villa Adriana, a complex and harmonious construction with urban architectural elements in a profound kinship with nature.

No precise records exist about the type of garden used in the Byzantine world. Nevertheless, for the relations, influences, and intercurrents between Persia and Byzantium, one can assume that the gardens of Constantinople (about which some information exists, but no adequate descriptions) were based from Persian prototypes. On the basis of the mosaics created at Constantinople's imperial palace during the fifth and sixth centuries, it is assured that the garden concept was functionally determined by the climate. Yet between terraces and tree-lined spaces, there was always an enormous pool with fountains and running water. This pool probably had a symbolic value, which the Christian religion subsequently

translated into the "font of life";[10] its iconography recurs in the figurative arts influenced by Byzantium. More certain is a late, though uncorroborated description made by Theodoros Metochitos (the lieutenant of Andronicus II) of his real estate holdings, which included various gardens containing ornamental waterworks.[11]

The recurrent Barbarian invasions ultimately led to the ruin of nearly all the Roman monuments, especially the gardens, which, be-

Roman garden from the map of Rome (detail). Engraving from 1574 by Stefano du Perac di Parigi. Printed in Rome by Jacobo De Rubeis at Santa Maria della Pace, Venice, Museo Correr.

ing among the frailest and most defenseless of human creations, require constant human care. Hence, during the Middle Ages, this landscaping tradition did not evolve, since Ro-

9. Grimal, "Mondo classico," 164.
10. R. Carità, "Oriente antico," *Enciclopedia universale dell'arte.* (Sansoni: Florence, 1958).
11. T. Metochites, "Description de son palais par lui-même," Carità, R., op. cit., p. 176.

man gardening had disappeared. The garden was now seen as an area of confinement, particularly in the monastic environment, which dictated the overall prototype. Reduced to a mere cloister within the monastery, the garden was surrounded by a colonnade, whose focal point was the uncovered central well. The monastic design was adopted by civil society; consistent with and depending on the given urban center, which was enclosed within the system of defensive walls, this layout persisted for centuries. The recurring cloistral pattern was conducive to ascetic meditation. Its functional character was rooted in the presence of the well, which became a symbol of the *fons salutis* (the font of salvation) in religious writings. This concept, developing into the notion of a fountain of youth,[12] passed into narrative literature, especially during the fifteenth century, when the fountain also became a familiar theme in the figurative arts.

The late thirteenth century and, even more so, the fourteenth century provided a rich and lively documentation of living conditions, which were more comfortable. Giovanni Villani, a chronicler of the early fourteenth century, wrote that the prosperous families, especially in Tuscany, "spent four months of the year in the country, in rich palazzi, towers, courtyards, and walled gardens." Villani's statement confirms that the Gothic garden was cut off from the surrounding landscape by a high, crenelated wall enclosing a natural microcosm. It was a sort of idyllic artificial paradise, suggesting the songs of May Day, the legends of knights or hermits—a typology linked to the religious sensibility of the *hortus conclusus,* as recorded by late Gothic painting. Here, the court gentlewoman assumes the image of the Madonna, and the garden symbolizes paradise. All this signaled an incipient laicizing of the religious emotion—a process typical of nascent humanism. According to documents, the fourteenth century had many gardens, with orchards, viridariums, and vegetable patches, "either to benefit from the fruits and vegetables or to refresh the souls,"[13] with the clear goal of intellectual leisure.

The Gothic garden, placed next to the house and locked in by walls, developed—as portrayed by Boccaccio,[14] around a cup-shaped fountain; the latter, generally made of white marble, stood at the center of a thick green meadow dotted with many varieties of flowers. Water continuously gushed from the fountain, gurgling into the elaborate jets, then vanishing into small hidden canals and resurfacing in small brooks around the edges of the field. The flower beds were subdivided and shaped into geometric forms by hedge-lined paths, which were covered by either pointed or barrel-vaulted arbors consisting of roses, clematis, or jasmine (the latter, together with the

Fountain of Youth. L. Dati, De Sphaere, late fifteenth century, miniature, Modena, Estense Library.

12. Argan, "Giardino e Parco: Problemi generali," 158.
13. Anonimus Ticinensis, "Liber de laudis civitatis Ticinensis," *Rerum Ital. Scrip* vol. 6, (Città di Castello, 1906), 1, 23. In Pavia, the garden built by Galeazzo Visconti had hazelnut espaliers around the walls, grape arbors, a fish pond, and a bathing pool. L. Dami, *Il giardino italiano* (Milan: Bestetti e Tuminelli, 1924), 1. See also: Puppi, "L'ambiente, il paesaggio e il territorio," 77.
14. G. Boccaccio, *The Decameron.* Introduction to the Third Day (Venice: Giolito de Ferrari, 1552), 207—209; *Idem,* ed C. Segre (Milan: Mursia, 1966), 176; G. Masson, *Italian Gardens,* (London: Thames and Hudson, 1966), 53.

F. Colonna, Poliphilo, Venice, Manuzio A., 1499, Engraving, Cherubim with grapevine pergola and fountain, Venice, Museo Correr.

lily, was brought by Crusaders returning from the Orient).

An exact description, with compositional and botanical details, is offered by Piero de' Crescenzi, of Bologna, in *Ruralium Commodorum* (*The Uses of the Countryside*), circa 1305. He gives the following advice: "[Gardens should have] tiny blades of grass; . . . There should be orchards and vegetable patches. The garden should be square in shape . . . and contain all manner of fragrant herbs, such as rue, sage, basil, sweet marjoram, mint, and the like. . . . There should also be flowers of every kind, such as violets, lilies, roses, etc. And if possible, the center of this garden should have a very bright fountain whose beauty arouses delight and mirth."

Giovanni da Prato talks about a detailed schematization of a fountain—the one in *Venere Cipriana*.[15] More than anything else, the paintings of the fourteenth and fifteen centuries, especially the miniatures, testify to the particular components of taste and organization in the Gothic garden, which was made up of various, often interdependent elements. There was a widespread use of aviaries, some of them large enough to contain trees, which provided better surroundings for the costly varieties of birds. Finally, next to the garden, there was not only a fish pond, but also a "bath" or square swimming pool,[16] as well as an orchard and a grove of olive trees, pines, laurels, and cypresses.

This was the period of a growing interest in nature, which was not merely viewed as a literary, idyllic, or decorative fact, but also

investigated scientifically. Not coincidentally, this era initiated the use and propagation of the *taccuina sanitatis* (health manuals) and herbariums listing every known variety of plant with its characteristics and therapeutic virtues. There was also great respect for the books of astrological botany derived from ancient Greek and Arabic prototypes.[17]

During the fifteenth century, urban gardens were still limited in size, and it is still the literary and artistic sources that give some idea of formal planting in that epoch. In Francesco Colonna's *Hypnerotomachia Poliphili* (1499), numerous woodcuts illustrate the botanical décor achieved by the imaginary garden of Cythera, which was seen as an ideal project; by now, the elements of bucolic architecture were prevailing together with bucolic sculpture.[18]

There is information that Cosimo the

F. Colonna, Poliphilo, Venice, Manuzio A., 1499, Engraving, Barrel-vault pergola, Venice, Museo Correr.

15. P. De' Crescenzi, *De Ruralium Commodorum*, Book VIII, Chapter I (Florence, 1478, published by Accademia della Crusca, Naples, 1724); Giovanni da Prato, *Il paradiso degli Alberti* vol 2 (Bologna, 1867), 31. See also: F. Fariello, *Architettura dei giardini*, (Rome: Ateneo, 1967), 231, and texts by Crescenzi, 44—45.
16. Dami, *Il giardino italiano*, 1.
17. M. Lupo, "Commento iconografico" *Erbario anonimo del XV secolo*, (Cassa di Risparmio di Venezia, 1980), 64.

Elder, in Florence, planted two small gardens, one on Via Larga and the other on San Marco. The latter, acquired by Clarice Orsini, the wife of Lorenzo de' Medici, was touted as "highly praiseworthy," perhaps partly in regard to the patronage ideals of Lorenzo the Magnificent and the definitive character he gave it, so that the garden could be considered the "first museum and first art academy in Europe."[19] The garden had to be planted according to *The Theories* of de' Crescenzi, who wanted "defense works of green trees similar to defense works of walls.[20] There were probably trellises of white roses, as in the Poggio garden in Cajano, described by Lorenzo.[21] Certainly the house, through the cryptoporticus, was linked to the garden, an open space rigorously articulated by paths lined with ancient statues. "A place where, according to Petrarch, solitude is emphasized, or where, rather, one can linger with preferred company. . . in the quest for humanist dignitas as opposed to the stress of political life."[22] Such were the intentions of Lorenzo the Magnificent when he explained, "I fled the harsh tempest of civic affairs in order to find a berth for my soul in a more tranquil harbor."[23] He may have been alluding to the peacefulness of Poggio's regal villa in Cajano, exalted with the plain name "Ambra" (amber) by Agnolo Poliziano and Lorenzo himself.

It was probably the late fifteenth century that brought the Oricellari Gardens, a country estate in the area known as Il Pantano, the bog, because of its adjacency to the Mugnone River. Here, Bernardo Rucellai offered hospitality to an intellectual elite that included such frequent guests as Machiavelli, Giovanni Corsini, Giovanni Cavalcanti, and others. This led to the famous Academy of the Oricellari Gardens (whereby Oricellari was a Latinization of Rucellai). When the Medici were driven from Florence in 1527, Bernardo Rucellai's son, Palla, was forced into exile, and the Oricellari Gardens were sacked. In 1608, they became the property of Gannantonio Orsini, and the garden was expanded on a grandiose scale, losing the Selva, the Forest, celebrated in the poems of Pier Crinito.[24]

Of all the Medici villas, the Careggi Villa, acquired in 1417, had a walled garden and a larger area reserved for cultivating ex-

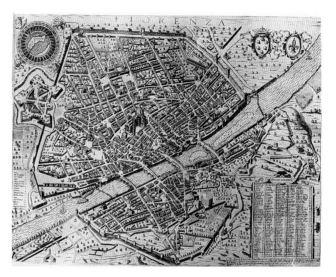

Above: *Perspective Map of Florence, Engraving, Venice, Museo Correr.*
Opposite: *L. Lotto, Secret Garden, detail of Christ's Farewell, 1521. Berlin, Gemaldegalerie.*

otic plants,[25] which, in 1480, were described in Latin verses by Alessandro Braccesi. The Medici garden can be seen as having an artistic kinship with the meadow in Botticelli's *Spring*, "in which viewers have identified a selection of plants that belong to mythology, but were probably culled from the Careggi flower beds."[26] On the other hand, the Fiesole Villa, built for Cosimo's son Giovanni de' Medici and located on a terrace, had the first example of a hanging garden.[27]

Around 1450, Nicolò V, the humanist pope, asked Leon Battista Alberti to remodel the papal palace in Rome; while the garden was treated peripherally, it nevertheless in-

18. F. Colonna, *Hypnerotomachia Poliphili*, (Venice: Manuzio, 1499. See also: G. Lepri, "Giardino," *Enciclopedia Treccani*, vol 17 (Milan: Tuminelli, 1933), 69.
19. E. Barfucci, "Il Giardino di San Marco," *Illustrazione*, (Florence, October 1940), 7. See also Karl Frey, *Michelangelo Buonarroti: sein Leben und seine Werke* vol 1 (Berlin: Curtius, 1907) 45.
20. P. De' Crescenzi, *De Agricultura;* (Venice: B. Sindoni, 1542). See also: G. Venturi, "Picta poâsis. Ricerche sulla poesia e il giardino dalle origini al Seicento," *Storia d'Italia*, Annali 5 (Turin: Einaudi, 1982), 677.
21. L. De' Medici, *Opere* ed. A. Simioni (Bari: Laterza, 1914). See also: F. Borsi and G. Pampaloni, *Ville e Giardini*. (Novara: De Agostini, 1984), 18.
22. G. Venturi, "Il giardino e la poesia," *Il giardino veneto*. (Milan: Electa, 1988), 227.
23. De' Medici, *Opere*, 18.
24. L. Passerini, *Curiosità storiche artistiche. Degli Orti Oricellari*, (Florence: Jouhaud, 1866), 30, 64; L. Ginori Lisci, *The Palazzi of Florence: Their History and Art* vol 1 (Florence: Giunti-Barbera, 1985), 211—217.

troduced architecture into the gardening system.

A few years later, in 1466, the court of Federico de Montefeltro welcomed the architect Luciano Laurana, who had been assigned the task of renovating the medieval castle of Urbino. The duke's apartments were given a terrace with a hanging garden, which was later described by the poet Bernardino Baldi, who resided at this court during the sixteenth century. He left an extremely precise idea of the rigorously geometric division of the area: "The squares created very wide paths and circular crossroads; at the center of each crossroads, there was a stone fountain, its huge basin, all of one piece, resting like a cup on its pedestal. This basin was encircled by three very light steps. To avoid producing a jet, the fountain gave off water not continuously, but only sporadically, depending on the occasion and the desire of the lords. The garden paths are all paved with huge square pieces of stones: the squares. . . like huge vases, contain soil. . . . Inserted into the walls surrounding the garden are stone seats, with ivy and jasmine growing behind them, forming a trellis on the wall."[28]

By the end of the fifteenth century, gardens were planned more rationally, with extremely geometric formal elements; this effort to recover the Latin tradition was based chiefly on literary documents, such as Petrarch's texts, that nostalgically recalled the Roman villas.

The medieval city had been opening up more and more toward the landscape. Often, the lord would move out to the country for given periods. Thus the villa, no longer meant as a rustic retreat for hunting and gardening,

25. L. Dami, "Il giardino toscano come opera d'arte," *Emporium* no. 232 (1914), 265; Dami, op. cit., 1924, pp. 9, 31, note 4.
26. A. Chastel, *Arte e umanesimo a Firenze al tempo di Lorenzo il Magnifico* (Turin: Einaudi, 1964), 160.
27. L. Dami, "Il giardino nel Quattrocento," *Dedalo* (1920—1921), 372; Dami, *Dedalo* (1924), 31, note 4.

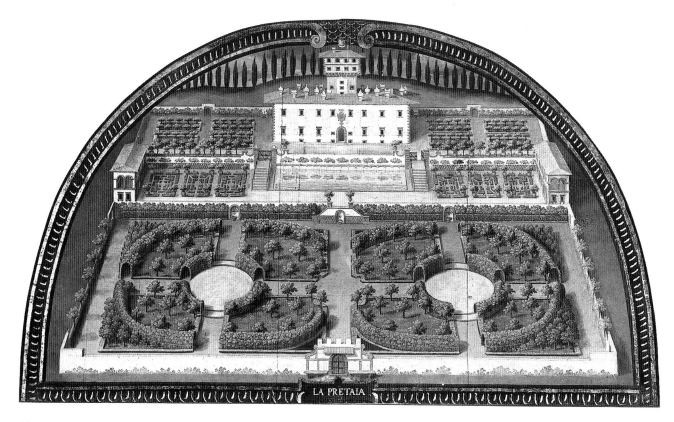

LA PRETAIA

Above: *Utens, View of the villa "La Pretaia," sixteenth century, Florence, Topographic Museum.*

Opposite: *L. Toeput, called Pozzoserrato (attributed), Garden with Pergolas, example of "ars topiaria," sixteenth century, Private Collection.*

was turned into a place of ideal nature, of pleasure and relaxation. The garden was no longer considered a kind of miniature nature, walled in and purely ornamental. Instead, evolving humanistically, it expanded with a vaster sense of nature and entered into a direct rapport with the architecture of the villa.[29] This process, continuing through the next century, showed a complex sense of luxury. Boccaccio, in the *Decameron*, and Bernardo Rucellai supply precise descriptions of the garden of Quaracchi; by 1480, this model of *ars topiaria*, illustrated in the *Zibaldone*, had grown so famous as to be considered a public treasure, so that the local inhabitants were willing to assume the expense of maintaining it.[30]

The architects focused on the symmetry of the lawns, planning gardens in terms of and in harmony with the buildings. A garden was diagrammed a priori with carefully reckoned spaces and a view that included the harmony of the trees. Thus began the architectural conception of the garden—albeit with an individual slant—as part of the return to classical

culture.

Tuscany may have been the first area to develop and affirm the idea of the architectural garden; here, artists like Alberti and Francesco di Giorgio codified the notion by applying constructional standards,[31] even "without a precise position," suggesting the use of "curiosities" to create a work of art.[32] Nevertheless, the elements that distinguish the garden of the late fifteenth century from its medieval forerunner must be emphasized. The Quattrocento garden was dominated by artistic aims, so that the house was linked to the planting area through a ground-level archway within the overall perspective. (A fine example of this is the Medici Villa at Carreggi, where Michelozzo introduced the loggia in 1487.) A

28. G. Bonarelli Modena, "I giardini all'italiana delle Marche," *Rassegna Marchigiana* vol 11 (1931), 163; G. Masson, *Giardini d'Italia*, (Milan: Garzanti, 1961).
29. Argan, "Giardino e Parco: Problemi generali," 158.
30. Dami, *Dedalo* (1920—21), 372, 373; Dami, *Dedalo* (1924), 33, note 7; G. Marcotti, *Un mercante fiorentino*, (Florence: Barbera, 1881), 72.

gradient was frequently remedied or at least masked by hanging gardens with ramps and stairs. The fountain was joined by further architectural elements, including pavilions (which Leonardo da Vinci had planned for the Sforza garden in Milan), grottoes, and the caverns recommended by Alberti: "In the grottoes of caverns, the ancients used to create hard or rugged surfaces by means of small pieces of pumice or sponge, and travertine. . . . I liked . . . a cave with a water fountain . . . and there was a surface containing various kinds of recesses and sea oysters."[33]

The decoration integrated ancient statues, marble seats and benches, huge flower vases, plus geometric or fantastic forms achieved by *ars topiaria*. The garden of Polifilo offers whimsical and highly elaborate examples together with designs for the flower beds[34]—illustrations that may have influenced artistic approaches toward the Renaissance garden, at least in the Veneto area.[35] Other particular elements were: sacred gardens (isolated and walled in perspectively); labyrinths; hills or lookout points; islets (so-called vivariums) in the pool or fish pond. The prevailing focus, however, was on coordinating a garden with the surrounding landscape, thereby creating a panoramic view.

By the end of the century, the garden typology had shifted toward the Cinquecento pattern, aiming at a perspective effect with nothing indefinite about it: "The composition

31. Carità, "Oriente antico," 178.
32. Dami, *Dedalo* vol 6 (1920—21), 178.
33. L.B. Alberti, L'architettura, chapter IX, VI, Venetia, Franceschi, F., 1565 (Milan: Polifilo, 1966).

of plane geometric forms in the plantings was no different from the wall surfaces that might be used by Brunelleschi or Luciano Laurana. Next came the solid geometric forms projected aloft and. . . tending to assume an architectural expression."[36]

The first garden with an architectural perspective was designed by Bramante in 1503, when Pope Julius II asked him to connect the Vatican Palace to the villa of Innocent VIII by way of the small court of the Belvedere. The architect recalled his Urbino training, the treatises of Leon Battista Alberti, the influence of Brunelleschi, and, above all, classical Roman architecture, which he could view directly. He managed to create a spectacular representation, using real structures and perspective suggestions.

All that now remains of Bramante's project is the plan itself. However, a drawing by Giovanni Dosi, preserved at the Uffizi in Florence, reveals that Bramante's link consisted of three levels. He reduced an incline of about three hundred meters to a gradient of twenty by creating two large horizontal terraces with a lawn and flower beds and intersected by

stairs, recesses, and fountains. These features, together with the lateral sloping of the architecture, provide a sense of continuity, culminating in a vast, crowning recess that was based on an entirely new concept. Thus was born the Italian garden, in which the architect wanted the "rationality of the wall architecture to have complete precedence over the tree architecture, which, however, is important as a color element."[37]

Bramante's canons were soon taken over, and varied, by Raphael in the designs commissioned by Cardinal Giulio de' Medici for the villa under Monte Mario (it was subsequently called the Villa Madama). The work, launched around 1510 and interrupted several times, was concluded, if not completed, in 1527 because of the Sack of Rome, which left the villa seriously damaged.

According to the basic conception, the "planted" terrace gardens, taking advantage of the sloping ground, were integrated into the

---

34. F. Colonna, *Hypnerotomachia Poliphili* (Venice: Manuzio, 1499), 16. See also: G. Masson, *Giardini d'Italia*, 62.
35. G. Pozzi and L.A. Ciapponi, "La cultura figurativa di F. Colonna e l'arte veneta," *Umanesimo europeo e Umanesimo veneziano* ed. V. Branca (Florence: Sansoni, 1963), 337, note 12; G. Venturi, *Le scene dell'Eden: Teatro, arte, giardini nella letteratura italiana*, 103.
36. Dami, *Il giardino italiano*, 13

Belvedere Garden of the Pontifical Palace, Rome, engraving by G.B. Falda, printed in Rome by G.I. Rossi, seventeenth century, A. Albrizzi Collection.

Virgilian peacefulness of the countryside. They were designed by Raphael, but with various elaborations; and Bramante's unifying concept may have been disregarded. However, the extant plans offer an excellent idea of the balanced grandeur of the ties between the diverse shapes used in the three "planted" terraces: square, circle, and ellipse. Furthermore, the curvilinear form of the stairs and the downward semi-circle behind the building produced a great ensemble effect, which was later expanded by the addition of Sangallo's nymphaeum.[38]

In this period throughout Italy, elaborate gardens were being created, partly inspired by an immense amount of construction. One reason for this development was the pagan and intellectual pleasure of living in a villa, as described by Machiavelli in a letter to Francesco Vettori in 1510.[39] Further reasons were utilitarian: the various demands made by the respective geographic zone. At any rate, it is certain that the appearance of the Cinquecento garden, often placed on a series of terraces ascending—partly through stairs—from the body of the villa, attained a great architectural significance. Its importance was equal to and, at times, even greater than that of the building to which it was attached; and the most outstanding architects devoted themselves to these projects, creating authentic masterpieces.

We can find many prestigious examples, some of which were subsequently reworked. Pesaro has the gardens of the ducal villas, the Imperiale, where, around 1527, Duchess Eleonora della Rovere asked Gerolamo Genga to design projects that could not always be carried out. "It is not enough to dream up beautiful fantasies, if they cannot be carried out for lack of skilled labor," as the architect himself explained. Nevertheless, he managed to link the Quattrocentesque villa laterally with the architectural coulisses in Roman style; they were theatrically placed on graded terraces, in which the plantings, consistent with *ars topiaria*, were distorted into boats and fantastic figures.[40]

There is also the Miralfiori Villa, which may have been built by the architect Filippo Terzi on the basis of designs by Genga's son.

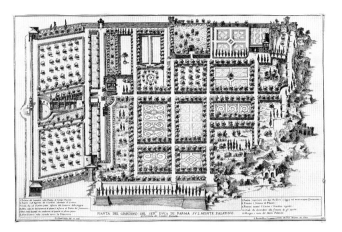

Map of the Garden of the Duke of Parma on the Palatine, Rome, engraving by G.B. Falda, printed by G.I. Rossi, seventeenth century, A. Albrizzi Collection.

In Rome, the gardens of Agostino Chigi's villa, known as La Farnesina, were planned between 1508 and 1511 by Peruzzi. Also in Rome, the garden of the Villa Giulia (1553) and the garden of the Villa Lante di Bagnaia were the works of Vignola, who had also devised "vineyard" compositions and small gardens with fountains and grottoes for the Villa Caprarola (1559). In Tuscany, on the slopes of Monte Morello, Nicolò Tribolo, at the behest of Cosimo I de' Medici, worked on the Villa Castello: he organized the surrounding garden, which was the first to follow an iconographic program celebrating the glory of the Medici and involving an allegorical exaltation of nature—themes conceived by Benedetto Varchi. Tribolo was responsible not only for the sculptures and the decoration, but also for the hydraulic system, which gathered spring water to feed the waterworks and the fish ponds.[41]

Indeed, water became a determining decorative feature, like the green hues of the

37. Carità, "Oriente Antico," 180. See also: J. Ackerman, "The Cortile del Belvedere," *Studi per la storia del palazzo Apostolico Vaticano* (Città del Vaticano, 1954); M. Azzi Visentini, *L'orto botanico di Padova e il giardino del Rinascimento* (Milan: Polifilo, 1984), 40—46.
38. Azzi Visentini, *L'orto botanico di Padova e il giardino del Rinascimento*, 52, 53.
39. N. Machiavelli, *Lettere* December 10, 1510, ed. F. Gaeta (Turin: UTET, 1984).
40. G. Gronau, *Documenti artistici urbinati*, (Florence: 1936), 137. Letter dated January 29, 1538; R. Varese, "Tiziano e i Della Rovere," *Notizie da Palazzo Albani* I (1976) 25, 25. The aim of *ars topiaria* was to create a topiary garden by pruning laurel, boxwood, or myrtle into various shapes. See also: G. Masson, *Giardini d'Italia*, 197, note 32.

Above: *Utens, Villa Castello, sixteenth century, Florence, Topographic Museum.*

Opposite: *Guerra, Fountains of the Bagnaia Gardens, drawing circa 1598, Vienna, Albertina Graphische Sammlung.*

plants. And finally, the sculptures of the fountains and "grottoes," often with fantastic characters, achieved decisive importance. The famous Tivoli Villa was designed after 1550 by Pirro Ligorio at the request of Cardinal Ippolito II of Este. Its garden slopes down over symmetrical terraces with elaborate waterworks and fantastic fountains, two of which, the Fontana dell'Ovato and the Fontana dei Draghi, are particularly extravagant. Today, the Villa d'Este, partly because of its optimal conditions, still offers the most complete example of the ideal Cinquecento garden. One can cite other examples (some of them lost) with the necessary stylistic and environmental differences: the Villa Doria in Genoa, in which the landscape element is oceanic; the Regio Parco in Turin, begun under Emanuele Filiberto; the one planned by Giulio Romano for the Palazzo Tè in Mantua.

The ambient "stage set" of the Boboli in Florence opens up like a horseshoe behind the Palazzo Pitti; the planted space huddles be-

tween two declivities rigorously divided into squares of dense vegetation. In front of the palace, at the center of the courtyard, there is a fountain, which, by way of a broad, rising avenue determines the perspective link with the pond on the upper terrace. This garden, designed by Tribolo in 1550 for Eleonora de' Medici, was probably completed by Ammannati together with fantastic decorations by Bernardo Buontalenti, which were perfectly in keeping with the Mannerist love of the bizarre. Hence, this garden was taken up again in the seventeenth century with a scenographic character.

However, the most singular idea of the sixteenth century was the park of the Villa di Pratolino in the hills of Fiesole. Planned in 1569 by Buontalenti, it was regarded in its time as a grandiose and princely eccentricity of

41. Mignani, D.: *Le ville medicee di Giusto Utens* (Florence: Arnaud, 1982), no. 26.

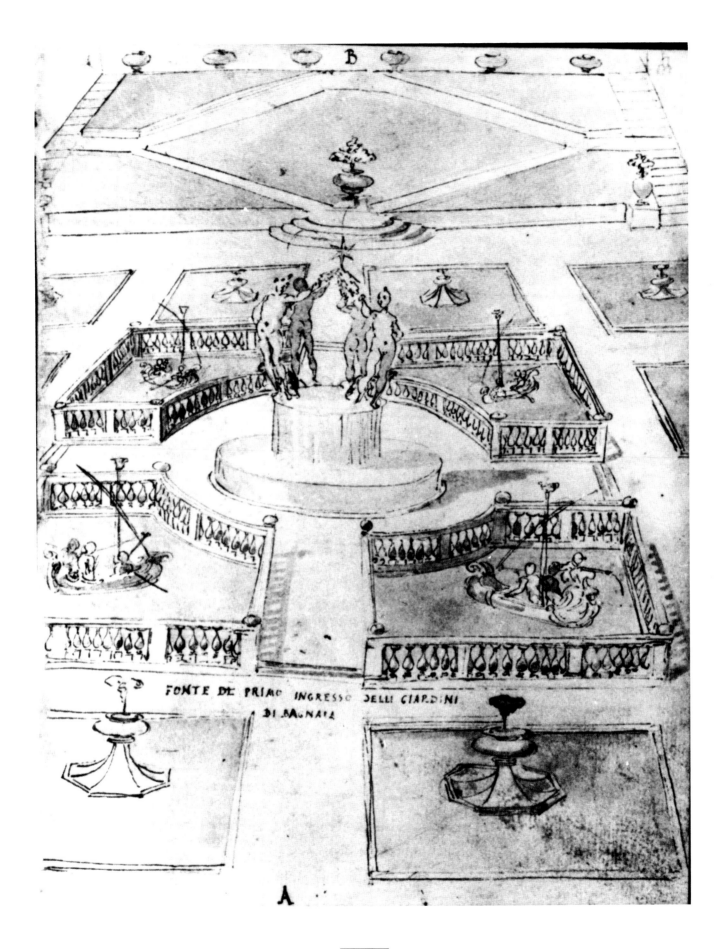

B

FONTE DE PRIMO INGRESSO DELLI CIARDINI
DI BAGNAIA

A

33

PRINCIPIO DELLA CATENA

FONTE DEL CIABATINO

C

BVLORI DELLA AVENSI   DELLA PLATA

Opposite: *Guerra, The Cobbler's Fountain at Bagnaia, drawing, sixteenth century, Vienna, Albertina Graphische Sammlung.*

Above: *Utens, Villa Pratolino, sixteenth century, Florence, Topographic Museum.*

Francesco I de' Medici. It was also celebrated in scores of poems, their rhetoric conveying the thrill of wonder that the park aroused in contemporaries. In this complex opus, the vast gardens adjacent to the villa were tenanted by bizarre statues, numerous fountains with water jets, and, finally, hosts of mechanical devices animating the architecture of the highly imaginative creation. In 1579, Gualtierotti described it as a competition between natural and artistic "grace," which "makes all the surroundings radiate with the splendor of new marvels."[42]

Later, in 1580, the French philosopher Montaigne was, despite himself, overwhelmed by the imposing beauty of the park. In his precise description, he points out the singularity of the man-made grottoes, which, placed inside the house, form the basic mainstay of the villa. He was also attracted to the "mobile" statuary and he observed that the musical sounds harmonized so well with the water jets; the latter were operated by mechanisms invented by Buontalenti,[43] and some of them gained value from being linked with Giambologna's space

sculptures. Because of its originality, Pratolino was renowned throughout the European courts, especially those in Germany. In 1565, Francesco I de' Medici had married Johanna of Austria, the daughter of Emperor Maximilian II; these family ties helped to spread knowledge of the innovativeness of this garden, which was widely imitated—and not only in Austria. In fact, while traveling to England in 1613, the Duke of Saxony saw the "Parnassus" of the gardens of Somers House and recognized their obvious derivation from Pratolino,[44] which was considered a prototype of European culture.[45] Furthermore, not only were the gardens of Pratolino conceived with the inexorable geometric rigor typical of the composition of Italian gardens, but they were also forerunners of the natural freedom that became characteristic in the seventeenth century,[46] anticipating not only the very concept of

---

42. R. Gualtierotti, *Vaghezze sopra Pratolino* (Florence, 1579). See also: Mignani, *Le ville medicee di Giusto Utens*, 73.

the park, but also several thematic notions of the "irregular gardens" so dear to William Kent.[47] The latter had visited Pratolino in 1714, and certain entries in his diary reveal that he was struck, above all, by the innovative grottoes: "Very fine Grotos (sic) adorn'd with shells and petrifical stone."[48]

In 1819, the park, radically transformed by Joseph Frietsch, began to resemble the English park; and after being totally abandoned, Buontalenti's villa was torn down in 1822.[49]

An emblematic exemplar is Bomarzo's Sacred Wood, planned in 1560 for Duke Vicino Orsini. Its implicit literary allusions, which were once linked to *Jerusalem Delivered*, have more recently been tied to passages in the first book of *The Divine Comedy* or to the journey to the inferno.[50]

Prints and paintings captured the images of famous gardens, some of which have been irremediably altered. Others, destroyed by men or by neglect, are known purely through historical texts; still others are evoked by literary settings, which were certainly factual in origin. This is probably true of the mythical portions in Ariosto's *Orlando Furioso*, which were "inspired by the great delight of the Belvedere" in Ferrara or the gardens of the Estensi, which surround the city—"virtually capturing the landscape—an important task of Ferrara's politics between the Quattrocento and the Cinquecento" and which emerged as "the court theater."[51]

In Veneto and Venice, the gardens developed a particular typology, which also distinguished the mainland villas from the Venetian palazzi.[52]

The physiognomy of the villa garden, which became known in the Cinquecento, bore the imprint of the small Tuscan-Roman garden with the stairway running down the central axis or the narrow path. However, the composition emphasized the natural element over the architectural element. Nevertheless, interest concentrated mainly on the beauty and grandeur of the edifice and not the garden. Palladio does not dwell overly on gardening. The villas in the Venetan countryside were constructed for a social class that favored a land investment on which to base its power. But the villa had to fulfill a chiefly practical function, be-

coming the focal point of the farming and the urbanization of the surrounding territory.

Hence, Palladio says that "the site is as pleasant and delightful as possible"—a reference to the landscape surrounding La Rotonda in Vicenza, which was tied to the woods on its southeastern side in order to camouflage the steep gradient of the hills, but, unlike the Tuscan-Roman gardens, with no preestablished architectural design.[53] Palladio also calls gardens and orchards "the souls and recreation

Guerra, Fantastic statues of the Bomarzo Garden, sixteenth century, drawing, Vienna, Albertina Graphische Sammlung.

43. M. De Montaigne, *Voyage en Italie par la Suisse et l'Allemagne*, (Paris). See also: Mignani, *Le ville medicee di Giusto Utens*, 73.
44. R. Strong, *The Renaissance Garden in England* (London, 1979), 90—91. See also: L. Zangheri, "I giardini d'Europa mappa della fortuna medicea nel XVI e XVII sec.," *Il giardino d'Europa* (Florence: Mazzotta, 1986), 89.
45. Zangheri, *Il giardino d'Europa*, 10.
46. L. Dami, *Il nostro giardino* (Florence: Le Monnier, 1921), 25—26.
47. L. Zangheri, "Lo splendore di Pratolino e Francesco I de' Medici," *Il giardino d'Europa*, 15.

of the villa."[54] In the gardening area, which is decorated with statuary, ground-level arcades supported by stairs achieve a seemingly classical appearance that actually tends to favor chiaroscuro over perspective. The horizon remains spacious, opening upon flat farmlands. Hedges frequently close off the garden, and sometimes an outside tree-lined path "seems to run all the way to the horizon."[55]

Scamozzi cites the gardens of Tuscan-Roman villas, but without great enthusiasm. He suggests a selection of perennials and annuals and, incredibly, he recommends the use of water jets, while the Venetan villa of the Cinquecento prefers the tranquility of the fish pond. The fountain also appears, but the element of water is not used as a lively decoration: the spurts are conspicuous without a rhythmic succession of cadences. The nymphaeum is generally located behind the villa, and aside from the placid brilliance of the water in the basin, it had refined stucco decorations (see Maser's Barbaro-Volpi Villa).

After the sack of Rome in 1527, Sansovino fled to Venice, where he became a curator of St. Mark's. Here he introduced the syntax of Tuscan-Roman classicism, applying it to the unified planning of Piazza San Marco. Around 1545, on the mainland, he constructed the Garzoni villa in Pontecasale, Padua. The chiefly agricultural function of the edifice, which was also set on level ground, did not provide for an adequate garden, and the entire architectural prospect opened upon a square, stagelike courtyard.

In the seventeenth century, Europe continued to favor Cinquecento Italian themes, but gardens grew in size, accentuating trees and a richer assortment of plants. These gardens were decorated with impressive sculptural groups, often surrounded by water and architecture—elements that produced a scenographic brightness partly through a greater compositional freedom. All these developments left behind the rules of symmetry that had dictated the garden typology of previous centuries. Hence, designers abandoned linear perspectives, and they left trees in their natural forms: *ars topiaria* gave way to the patch of woods. New gardens were planted not just throughout Italy, with Rome still in the lead, but also throughout Europe.

Noteworthy are the following: the gardens of the Villa Doria Pamphily, which have remained intact in their area, but with changes in the original design; the garden of the Villa Corsini, Florence, designed by Silvani; the Collodi garden near Lucca; the garden of the Poggio Imperiale School, Siena, designed by Giulio Parigi in 1622; and others. The year 1622 also brought the famous garden of Isola Bella, on Lago Maggiore in Lombardy; it was initiated by Carlo Borromeo and planned in collaboration with various architects.

It was not always the most famous gardens that were damaged, because the style

Villa Morosini at Santa Anna, drawing by M. Cochin, engraving by M. Desbois, 1683, Venice, Museo Correr.

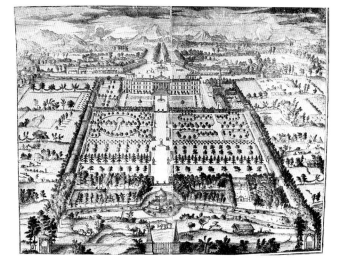

48. K. Woodbridge, "William Kent and Landscape Gardening: A Reappraisal," *Apollo* no. 100. (August, 1974), 126—127.
49. Zangheri, L.: "L'arteficio paesaggistico nel parco di J. Frietsch," *Il Giardino d'Europa*, 122
50. Maiorano, G.: "Il bosco sacro di Bomarzo, un mosaico da ricomporre, in: *Le dimore storiche* (Rome: L'economia, 1990), 10. See also: G. Guerra: *Libri di immagini*, copyright Comune di Modena, 1978.
51. G. Venturi, *Le scene dell'Eden: Teatro, arte, giardini nella letteratura italiana*, 105, 106, 110. The Belvedere villa with the garden was destroyed along with most of the Estensi gardens when Ferrara was taken over by the Vatican in 1598. A papal fortress was erected on the site.
52. I. Chiappini di Sorio, *Introduction to The Gardens of Venice* (New York: Rizzoli, 1989).
53. R. Cevese, *Ville della provincia di Vicenza* (Milan: SISAR, 1971), 31.
54. A. Palladio, *I Quattro libri di Architettura* Book I, Chapter XII; C. Semenzato, *La Rotonda*. (Schio: Pasqualotto, 1980), 14.
55. M.T. Cruciani-Boriosi, "Il giardino veneto," *Antichità viva* (1966), 50.

was altered by the superimposition of styles; nevertheless, we can gain a notion of how the garden of the early seventeenth century, partly under the impact of literature, acquired an emblematic significance and was influenced by the theater. The use of "mechanical effects" achieved fantastic results, as on the stage. In fact, water jets and unexpected terrifying noises in the grottoes were produced by mechanical devices. The fantastic decorations went back to the inventions of Buontalenti, who, inside the grotto of the garden of Boboli, had included figures having lively attitudes, but also supporting the grotto itself.[56]

The seventeenth-century garden initiated the "water theater," as seen in the villa of Pietro Aldobrandini, the nephew of Clemente VIII. Here, Oliviero Olivieri, the fountain attendant at the Villa d'Este, had designed a waterfall that plunged over basins and cascades, winding up in the semi-circle of the theater. The fountain of Atlas stood at the center of the theater and the lateral niches had musical hydraulic devices.

There were also arboreal amphitheaters—for instance, at the Villa Reale of Marlia (today Pecci Blunt) in Lucca; this was demonstrated by the architecture of boxwood hedges and cypresses. Other amphitheaters were built out of stone, as in the Boboli, and added to that garden in that era. Even today, that garden displays an exemplary relationship between nature and architecture—a rapport made even more sumptuous by the rich collection of statues (most of them coming from Pratolino), the gray granite basin (which used to be at the Caracalla Baths in Rome), and the Egyptian obelisk. All these elements were fused in a setting consistent with the vegetation and the architecture of the house.

In contrast, the garden of La Gamberaia had a classical design that visually converged in the central fountain through rectilinear paths. The original structure, which goes back to 1610, is attributed to Ammannati. It made no concession to the bizarre; the architect, taking into account the unevenness of the terrain, created a symmetry of—still extant—stairs and balustrades, which he tied to the superb arboreal compositions. This produced a more balanced, more harmonious perspective in a garden constituting a typical aspect of the Italian tradition. It was closed off by the plant amphitheater, which was created by means of *ars topiaria* and fused with the natural backdrop of the lower landscape.

In Veneto, the seventeenth-century garden that was the most unusual in its formation and location was the Barbarigo, now Pizzoni, in Valsanzibio di Garzignano on the outskirts of Padua. It still exists today. The original garden of the villa was expanded in 1678 by annexing a contiguous area and overcoming the gradient of the terrain through a short flight of stairs connecting the two levels. Next, a water permit was obtained for the alleged purpose of running a mill; but actually, the water was used in a complex network of subterranean pipes and connecting basins subordinated to the arboreal design—with spectacular effects. The implementation of the initial project was

Ammannati, Fountain with statue ensemble for the Pratolino, drawing by G. Guerra, sixteenth century. In 1589 the fountain was moved to the Boboli Gardens. Vienna, Albertina Grapische Sammlung.

CONCERTO POETICO DI STATVE POSTO IN ASPETTO DEL PALAZZO A PITHI FATTO PER INTENTIONE DI METERLO A PRATOLINO

Villa La Gamberaia, Florence, engraving, L'uccelliera (The Aviary), Florence, Private Collection.

illustrated in 1702 by Domenico Rossetti with engravings by Campana.

The main entrance to the property is on the side and it is connected to the transversal axis of the garden. Barbarigo had designed a waterway that could be reached through various canals, which are no longer used today. The landing place is still a monumental structure, embellished with statues and niches and overlooking the surface of the so-called bath of Diana.

However, a person arriving by boat or on foot did not have an immediate perspective view of the country house according to Renaissance canons. The sight was shaped not only by the arboreal structures that lead to avenues intersecting with obvious geometric rigor, but also by other singular creations involving nature. Furthermore, even today, the hidden *jeux d'eaux* ensnare the unsuspecting visitor. The labyrinth, delineated by boxwood hedges, culminates in a central belvedere with a small temple; and, starting in the seventeenth century, this maze had the illusory function of allowing visitors to get lost and to indulge in amorous playfulness. Valsanzibio's multivalent plans, involving prearranged architectural and vegetable elements, unite into a single design, resembling a stage set.[57]

After the decline of machinery effects in the late seventeenth century, architecture still prevailed in highly elaborate forms that were, however, mellowed by the surrounding freedom of nature.[58] The characteristics of the baroque garden were understood and restated by a creator of new and renewed designs:

André Le Nôtre, the "gardener" par excellence. Born in France in 1613, he studied architecture and painting with Vouet; soon, in 1637, he became superintendent general of the buildings of King Louis XIV. Extraordinarily educated, he invented the so-called French garden, which dominated Europe throughout the eighteenth century. Le Nôtre, acquainted with Bramante's theories, placed the villa at the center of the garden to keep from scattering the latter. Adding simple forms, he framed the composition with geometrical borders that stretched out in vast, level spaces, the goal being to tie in the surrounding nature without a precise limit. As Margherita Azzi Visentini notes, this produced an allegorical form evoking the absolute power of Louis XIV.[59] Furthermore, long rectangles, their short sides gently curving, enclosed flower beds—"embroideries" created with a diversity of flowers; while very low borders of contrasting plants, perhaps inspired by the sculptural decorations of manor houses, produced a precise and calibrated perspective effect, increasing the overall spatial illusion. The trees, linked in space, cast mysterious shadows on the paths, while the water, motionless in huge basins, reflected the light:[60] together these elements wove into a

56. M.T. Cruciani-Boriosi, "La realizzazione barocca del giardino e la sua parziale discendenza dalla contemporanea scenografia," *Antiquità viva* (1963), 15. See also: G. Venturi, "I 'dolci inganni': l'idea del giardino nella letteratura poetica del Seicento," *Notizie da palazzo Albani* no. 1-2 (1983), 213.
57. L. Fontana, *Valsanzibio* (Padua: Bertoncello, 1990), copyright by Fabio Pizzoni Ardemani, Valsanbizio.

PRIMO VIALE DEGL' AGRVMI CON FONTANE E SCHERZI D'ACQVA NEL GIARDINO DELL'ECCELLENTISSIMA CASA BARBARIGO POSTO IN VAL SAN ZIBIO TRA COLLI EVGANEI

D. Rossetti, Garden and Avenue of the Citrus Trees at Valsanzibio, engraving in The Farms and Gardens of the Most Excellent Casa Berbarigo, Verona, 1702, Venice, Museo Correr.

continuous counterpoint of delicate pictorial sequences.

Le Nôtre's style, crossing the French borders, spread throughout Europe, replacing the Italian legacy. The gardens at Versailles and at the royal palace of Turin offer almost intact examples of Le Nôtre's work as a function of the theatricality of the court;[61] they mirror the enthusiasm with which his style was accepted throughout Europe, even after his death. It extended as far as Vienna, albeit somewhat varied. In 1752, near Caserta, Italy, Luigi Vanvitelli built the palace, modeling it after Versailles and designing a masterpiece of garden art behind the palace on a terrain of some hundred acres, part hilly, part flat, with a vast prospect created by waterfalls, fish ponds, and fountains.

In England, the French style had little impact, even though Le Nôtre was asked by Charles II to personally design the parks of Greenwich and St. James. Meanwhile, a British architect, William Kent, inspired by the poet Alexander Pope, created the so-called English garden. This "landscape garden" was highly successful during the period of Romanticism,[62] partially thanks to the theories of Jean-Jacques Rousseau, who advocated a return to primitive simplicity. The composition of the English garden, which the German poet Schiller referred to as the "aesthetic garden," opposed rigorous geometrical symmetry even in the trees, allowing them to develop naturally. Hence, "regularity," an architectural stan-

58. M.T. Cruciani-Boriosi, "La realizzazione barocca del giardino e la sua parziale discendenza dalla contemporanea scenografia," 26.
59. M. Azzi Visentini, *L'orto botanico di Padova e il giardino del Rinascimento*, 68.

dard, had to yield to nature.[63]

The new style circulated rapidly. Of particular significance is the fact that in 1782, a garden following the new back-to-nature movement was set up next to the park in Caserta; but ultimately, its design was a mere imitation. The nature garden, with its predominantly pictorial goals, was made up of small lakes, phony ravines, vestiges of classical statuary, and small temples and shrines. It included landscape foreshortenings, plus allusions to the love of chinoiserie, which was due chiefly to the influence of Chinese philosophy. Furthermore, there were winding paths with large trees, especially weeping willows, and extensive lawns covered with dazzlingly verdant and velvety grass.

The English garden, inevitably spelling the end of the Italian garden, was accepted even at the Austrian court, which left a token of its rule in Lombardy. 1778 saw the construction of the Monza villa, "whose gardens represented the end of the century and also—at least for the fifteen years of the Napoleonic era in the nineteenth century—was a model. . . of compromise between the Italian and the English garden, which could more aptly be called a 'landscape garden.'"[64] Around 1779, a singular example was planned at Cinisello Balsamo by Count Ercole Silva, a theorist on the art of the English garden and a nephew of the illustrious botanist Donato Silva; the latter, who had introduced Milan to exotic plants, was considered by Pietro Verri to be the first scholar of exotic botany.[65] For Ercole Silva, the garden had to copy the beauties of nature, so that "man could tranquilly enjoy the boons of rustic life and the renascent delights of the seasons." For this reason, as Venturi observed, Silva accepted an artificial nature, because it was guided by art with an apparent freedom, and the gardener-artist had to be close to the painter, but far from the architect.[66]

Florence also accepted the English style, though substituting certain plants typical of Tuscan gardens and omitting the peculiar perspective rigor of the Italian Renaissance, which had dominated Europe for some two centuries. The "English" influence triggered harsh criticism, especially in 1831, when the architect Luigi de Cambray-Digny applied radical innovations to the historic gardens of Oricellari.[67] At the same time, the Torrigiani gardens were designed at Porta Romana,[68] with all the components of the English garden; as Edith Wharton points out, this involved particular features that were not adapted to the local climate and did not fit in with the Tuscan vegetations—for instance, the English lawn.[69]

During this era, the focus on an Italian setting linked to the surroundings was demanded, perhaps even more strongly, by certain British residents in Tuscany. Arthur Acton redesigned the garden of the Villa La Pietra, which had been designed according to the English style when it belonged to the Capponis, altering its chromatic and architectural values. As soon as the property became Acton's, it was changed back into the Italian style.[70] A different route was taken by Stibbert around 1884, at his Montughi residence, where he created an English garden consistent with the art nouveau architecture of the villa, which was remodeled and enlarged by the architects Giuseppe Poggi and Gaetano Fortini to house the celebrated art collection.[71]

The new stylistic trend of the garden expressed the taste for natural and causal freedom, liberating it from geometric constriction. The style then moved to America, where parks and gardens were being laid out; the compositional use of traditional motifs indicated an artificially re-created freedom that nevertheless respected the geological structure—for example, at the Villa Torlonia in Rome.

In the twentieth century, the garden areas on the outskirts of huge urban centers are meant to reestablish the balance between man and his surroundings. This trend has been especially important in northern countries like

60. Carità, "Oriente antico," 186.
61. Venturi, Le scene dell'Eden: Teatro, arte, giardini nella letteratura italiana, 211.
62. Carità, "Oriente antico," 188.
63. Assunto, Paessaggio e l'estetica: Concetto di giardino vol. 3, 225—226.
64. G. Venturi, Introduction toSilva, E.: Dell'arte dei giardini inglesi (MilanL: Longanesi, 1976), 7—8.
65. E. Silva, Dell'arte dei giardini inglesi (Milan: Vallardi, 1913), edited by G. Venturi (Milan: Longanesi, 1978).
66. Venturi, Introduction toSilva, E.: Dell'arte dei giardini inglesi 20; Venturi, Le scene dell'Eden: Teatro, arte, giardini nella letteratura italiana, 88.

Sweden, Norway, Denmark, and Holland. But traditional garden design has changed irreversibly, and the customary features, such as paths, fences, statues, and fountains, have been replaced by swimming pools on the lawns, verandas, and terraces with plants. The latter are integrated into the interior by the architecture itself, as in Le Corbusier's designs for the home of Carlos de Beistegui on the Champs Elysées in Paris.[72]

"Captured" nature became a functional element in the design of the garden as well. For instance, in Frank Lloyd Wright's residential designs, strongly influenced by Japanese gardens, he employed light to create a kinship between architecture and nature, which he saw as an intrinsic part of the composition. This goal was realized at Fallingwater, 1936, in which the architect used the surrounding landscape as a structural element.

Translated from the Italian by Joachim Neugroschel

67. Passerini, *Curiosità storiche artistiche. Degli Orti Oricellari*, 30, 32. See also: L. Zangheri, "L'arteficio paesaggistico nel parco di J. Frietsch," 122.
68. Ginori Lisci, *The Palazzi of Florence: Their History and Art*, 91.
69. Edith Wharton, *Italian Villas and their Gardens* (London: John Lane, The Bodley Head, 1904).
70. L. Zangheri, *Ville della Provincia di Firenze. La città* (Milan: Rusconi, 1989), 133. See also: M. Agnelli, *Giardini Italiani* (Milan: Fabbri, 1987), 130—133.
71. H. Russel Robinson, *Il Museo Stibbert*. Introduction by G. Cirri (Florence: Cassa di Rispiarmio; Milan: Electa).
72. M. Chiarini, "Giardini e parchi del XIX e XX secolo," *Enciclopedia universale dell'Arte* vol 6 (Florence: Sansoni, 1954), 188, 190.

Villa Doccia, Florence, owned by Marquis Ginori, engraving in Lo stato presente di tutti i paesi e popoli del mondo, vol. XXI, G.B. Albrizzi, Venice, 1759, p. 91, Venice, Museo Correr.

*View of Florence, engraving, late eighteenth century,
drawing by M.S. Giampiccoli and by the architect Corbelier,
Venice, Museo Correr.*

La Real Villa di LAPPEGGI, *luogo*

Villa Lampeggi, Florence, engraving in Lo stato presente di tutti
i paesi e popoli del mondo, *vol. XXI, G.B. Albrizzi, Venice, 1759,
p. 99. Venice, Museo Correr.*

...delizia de' Gran Duchi di Toscana

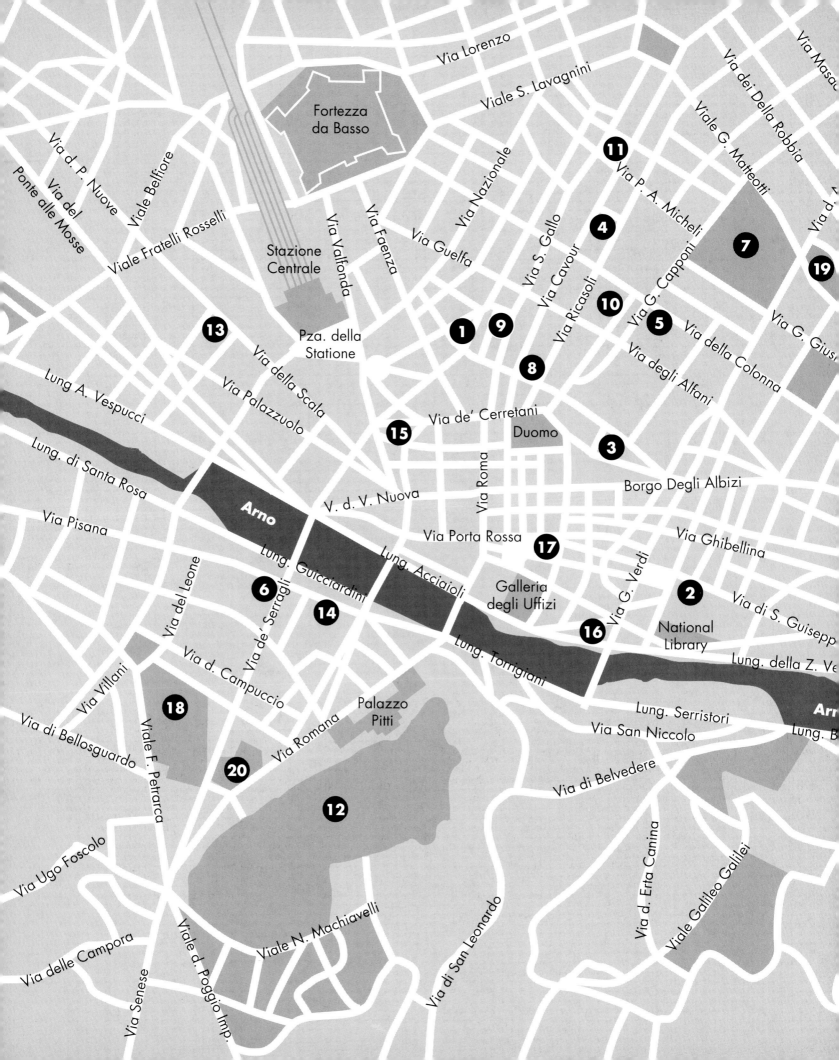

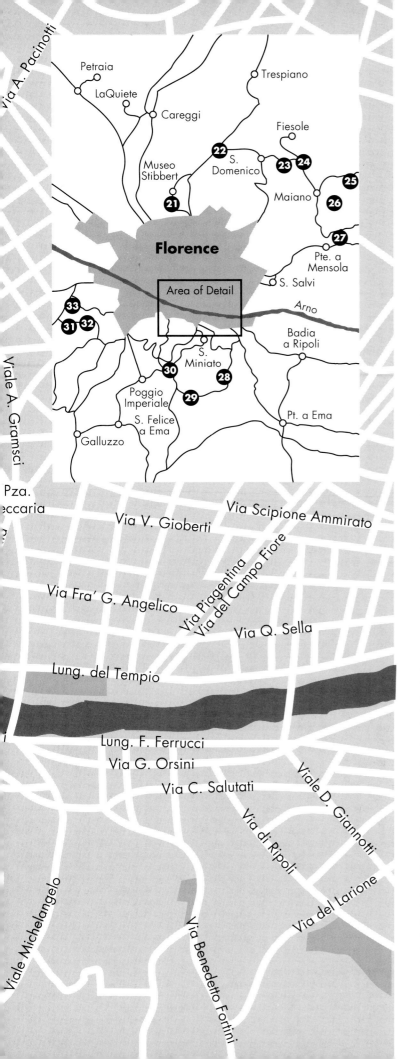

The locations of the gardens included in this book are indicated on the map presented here. While many of these gardens are private, some are open to the public or can be visited with the permission of their owners.

1. *Cloister of San Lorenzo. Piazza San Lorenzo. Open to the public.*
2. *Cloister of the Church of Santa Croce. Piazza Santa Croce. Open to the public.*
3. *Cloister of the Museo Firenze com'era. Via dell'Oriuolo. Open to the public.*
4. *Cloister of the Convent of San Marco. Piazza San Marco. Open to the public.*
5. *Cloister of the Spedale degli Innocenti. Piazza SS. Annunciata. Open to the public.*
6. *Palazzo Feroni. Via de'Serragli. Private. The garden can be seen through the gates of the palace.*
7. *Palazzo Incontri (The German Institute). Via Giusti. The garden can be visited with the permission of the institute.*
8. *Palazzo Medici Riccardi. Via Cavour. Open to the public.*
9. *Palazzo Ginori Lisci. Via de'Ginori. Private.*
10. *Palazzo Budini-Gattai (Prefecture of Florence). Piazza SS. Annunciata. The garden can be visited with permission of the Prefecture.*
11. *Palazzo Pandolfini. Via San Gallo. Private. The garden can be seen through the gates of the palace.*
12. *Palazzo Pitti and Boboli Garden. Piazza Pitti. Open to the public.*
13. *Palazzo Orti Oricellari (Cassa di Risparmio di Pisa Bank). Via degli Orti Oricellari. The garden can be visited with the permission of the bank.*
14. *Palazzo Frescobaldi. Via S. Spirito. Private. The garden can be visited with the permission of the Frescobaldi family.*
15. *Palazzo Antinori. Piazza Antinori. Private. The garden can be visited with the permission of the owners.*
16. *Palazzo Malenchini. Via de'Benci. Private.*
17. *Palazzo Gondi. Piazza S. Firenze. Private.*
18. *Villa Torrigiani. Via del Campuccio. Private.*
19. *Cimitero degli Inglesi. Open to the public.*
20. *Villa Annalena. Via de'Serragli. Private.*
21. *Museo Stibbert. Via Stibbert. Open to the public.*
22. *Villa La Pietra. Via Bolognese. Private.*
23. *Villa Medici. Stradone di Fiesole, Fiesole. Private.*
24. *Villa Ferragamo. Fiesole. Private.*
25. *Villa San Michele (Hotel San Michele). Fiesole. Open to guests of the hotel. The garden can be visited with the permission of the hotel's owners.*
26. *Villa La Gamberaia. Settignano. Private. The garden can be visited with the permission of the owners.*
27. *Villa I Tatti. Settignano. The garden can be visited with the permission of Harvard University.*
28. *Villa Marchi. Piazza Calda, Santa Margherita a Montici. Private.*
29. *Convent of San Domenico. Via San Domenico, Arcetri. Private.*
30. *Villa Capponi. Via Plan de'Giullari, Plan de'Giullari, Arcetri. Private.*
31. *Villa L'Ombrellino. Private. The garden can be visited with the permission of the owners.*
32. *Torre di Bellosguardo. Bellosguardo. The garden can be visited with the permission of the Hotel Torre di Bellosguardo.*
33. *Villa La Limonaia. Bellosguardo. Private.*

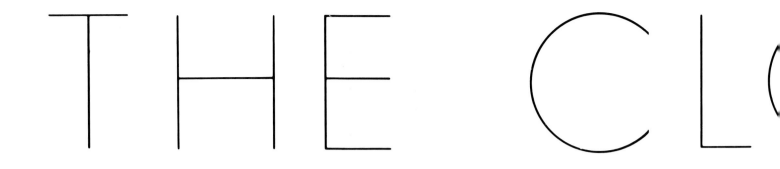

THE CLO

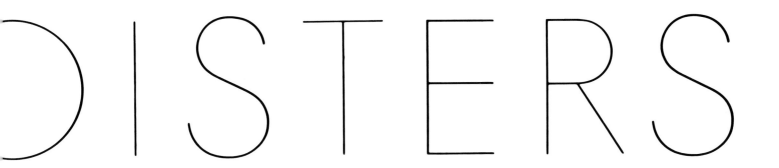

First cloister, Santa Croce.

GARDENS OF
THE CLOISTERS
inspirations
from nature and
architecture

The gardens of the ancient churches were some of the earliest designed gardens. Walls, loggias, or *portici* brought some sense of order and character to these protected areas that provided the religious communities with vegetables, flowers, and a place for contemplation. In Florence, the cloister gardens are particularly refreshing enclaves of green trees and shrubs. The light and the beauty of nature contrasts with the cool interiors of the huge basilicas and vaulted churches filled with breathtaking art. Florentines refer to the strong reaction to viewing so much great art in the churches and galleries as the "Stendahl syndrome." While on an art tour of Florence, the famous writer Stendahl reportedly fainted with ecstasy at the glory of the art he was viewing at a gallery and had to be carried outside for fresh air.

Like the churches, the convents and their cloisters were often planned by Italy's most accomplished architects. Brunelleschi, Michelangelo, Michelozzo, and others have given Florence a series of glorious colonnaded gardens. Today, the sparse plantings begin with simple panels of grass, some punctuated with ancient trees or statues. Quite often there are clipped hedges, sometimes in parterre patterns. If the cloister is paved it may be enlivened with a few containers of seasonal flowers or potted citrus trees. The architecture always dominates, bringing to the space a beauty that lifts the spirit, and reminds one of the greatness of God's gifts through man: "To make known to the sons of men his mighty acts, and the glorious majesty of his kingdom" (Psalms 145).

Angels in the coat of arms of the Serragli family herald spring at the Museo di Firenze com'era. The museum is housed in the fifteenth-century Convent of the Oblates that served as the hospital, Spedale Nuovo. A picturesque double loggia borders a square of green, a welcoming garden near the Santa Maria del Fiore cathedral. Cedars and oleanders shade carpets of grass dotted with wildflowers.

San Lorenzo, the extraordinary church of the Medicis, was the work of the masterful architect Brunelleschi, and the cloister was built in his style. The important Biblioteca Mediceo-Laurenziana adjacent to the cloister was planned by Michelangelo, as was the splendid family chapel attached to the church. In the heart of Florence, these magnificent structures house the Medici tombs and many of the family's most glorious treasures. The cloister contains a simple boxwood parterre that centers on an orange tree. A border of azaleas is in spring bloom.

53

An early restoration of the thirteenth-century church of San Marco was attributed to the architect Michelozzo. He also designed the Convent of San Marco used by the Dominican friars of Fiesole. This religious community included the reformer Savonarola, and the celebrated painter Fra' Angelico, so called because of the angelic quality of the figures in his frescoes that enrich the church and monk's cells. There are two cloisters: one dedicated to Sant'Antonio, and a larger one, designed by Michelozzo, devoted to San Domenico. A statue of this saint stands in the cloister, which is patterned with pebbled paths, giant palms, and clipped box.

Brunelleschi is responsible for a superb example of early Renaissance architecture, the foundling hospital, Spedale degli Innocenti, which was commissioned by the guild of silk merchants and tailors in 1419. An incredibly beautiful loggia, decorated with della Robbia terra cottas of babes in swaddling clothes, faces the Piazza della Santissima Annunziata. Sheltered inside, and opening into the church of Santa Maria degli Innocenti, is a cloister, also designed by Brunelleschi, that is decorated with symbols of the hospital's mission to save abandoned children—"the innocents."

THE

MEDICI

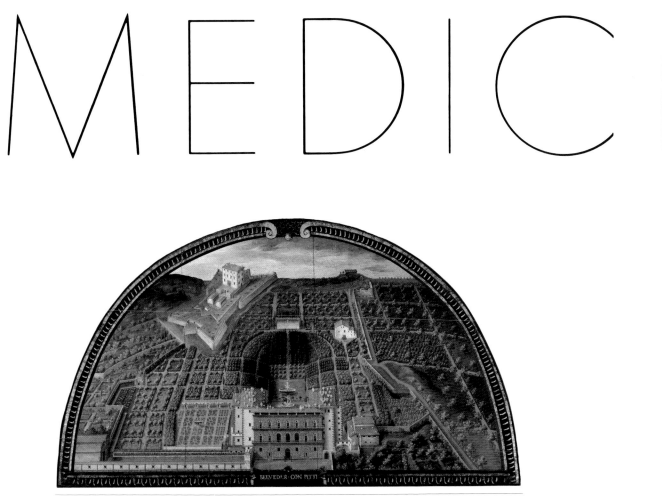

Lunette of Boboli by Utens.

PALAZZO MEDICI-RICCARDI

a historic courtyard sculpture garden

Palazzo Medici-Riccardi is an architectural triumph by Michelozzo, built for Cosimo the Elder. It was enlarged during the early sixteenth century, with some of the work attributed to Michelangelo. The courtyard is typical of the Florentine palaces of the period. Baroque figures and potted lemon trees are set off by panels of grass.

Overleaf: *The Riccardi key from the family crest is depicted in the decorative pebbled walk of the second courtyard. A wisteria-covered pergola on top of the grand loggia offers shade. From the small pool: the refreshing sound of splashing water.*

This extraordinary palace, for centuries home to two powerful families, the Medici and the Riccardi, was built for Cosimo the Elder about 1465. He chose a design by Michelozzo, after rejecting a plan by Brunelleschi which he considered too sumptuous and believed would cause envy. In his book on Florence, Luciano Berti writes: "Cosimo always regarded envy as a danger to be avoided: he used to say that envy was a dangerous weed which must be allowed to dry up and not be watered." The palace is a large square structure with a tremendous classical cornice, fourteenth-century divided windows, and a heroic first-floor colonnade inspired by Brunelleschi. According to historian Leonardo Ginori Lisci, it "represents the first example of a private residence worthy of a rich Renaissance gentleman." Scholars of architecture consider it a masterpiece, the model for other important palaces of the period.

Michelangelo, Donatello, and Benozzo Gozzoli added to the splendor and treasured contents. Even the courtyards were gardens of grandeur. The second courtyard was filled with topiary in exotic shapes, including animals and ships.

After the murder of Duke Alessandro in 1537, the young Cosimo I decided Palazzo Vecchio would be a safer place to live so he removed himself and all the family possessions. It wasn't until the mid-seventeenth century that the Riccardis, an immensely rich merchant family, bought the palace and began to restore the glory of early Medici princes. During the eighteenth century, changes were made to both courtyards. The first arcade was walled in. Baroque frames, inscriptions, and Roman fragments were added. Today, Palazzo Medici-Riccardi houses the prefecture of Florence and a small Medici museum.

At some point in time, a stone head of Marchese Francesco Riccardi was attached to a classical stone figure and placed in a niche in the second courtyard. He still surveys the scene of baroque figures and potted lemon trees.

PALAZZO GINORI LISCI

a family garden for nearly five hundred years

The illustrious Ginori family is most known around the world for the flowered porcelain produced by the famous Doccia factory started by Carlo Ginori in 1737. Services and objets d'art decorated with the flowers and foliage that still brighten the gardens in and around Florence are treasured by porcelain collectors and museum curators. Some of these same flowers flourish in the small parterre garden surrounded by Palazzo Ginori in the center of the city.

Late in the thirteenth century the Ginori family moved to Florence from Calenzano, and soon took an active part in government, giving the Republic five Gonfaloniers of Justice and twenty-six Priors. The palace was built between 1516 and 1520, an important addition to three houses on property owned by Carlo. It is thought the structure was designed by the prolific architect Baccio d'Agnolo, and there is evidence that d'Agnolo knew and worked for Ginori.

Carlo left the palace to his nephew, Leonardo, who married Caterina Soderini. It was her sister's son, Lorenzino, who involved the family in the Medicean tragedy of 1537. Lorenzino lured Duke Alessandro to his house with the promise of a tryst with his young aunt, and, with the help of a hired assassin, murdered the Duke.

Late in the seventeenth century Senator Ginori enlarged the palace to include a house and small garden facing Via della Stufa. Talented young architect Lorenzo Merlini was called in to design and oversee the work that was started in 1691 and completed in 1730. The central façade with two loggias, the two lateral façades, the gate wall with niches, and the narrow terrace with balustrade that runs along all four sides were designed by Merlini. Still standing in the center of the garden is the fountain, fashioned in the French manner, by Antonio Ferri.

Palazzo Ginori remains the seat of the Ginori-Lisci branch of the family—its beauty and refreshing green garden delight all who visit there.

A pergola covered with yellow Chinese roses, Rosa banksia lutescens, which flourish in Florence, is a fragrant sunscreen for the courtyard at Palazzo Ginori Lisci. Privet edging separates pebbled paths from panels of grass. A small fig tree and other plants are placed randomly, adding interest and more green to the view from the palace windows.

Overleaf: The façade and ground plan, drawn by Giovan Filippo Ciacchi and dated 1730. View of the courtyard designed by Lorenzo Merlini and built in the late seventeenth century.

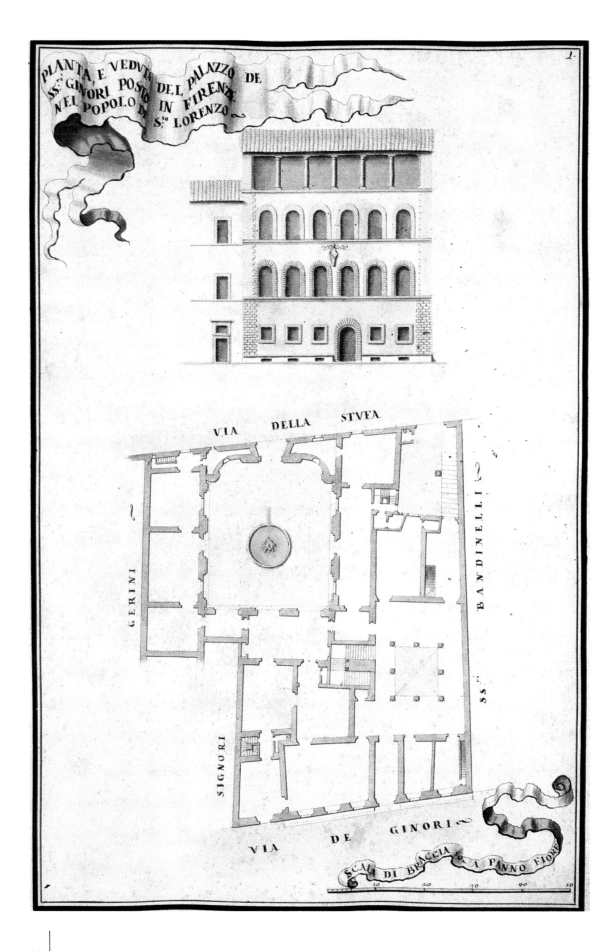

PLANTA E VEDVTA DEL PALAZZO DE
SS. GINORI POSTO IN FIRENZE
NEL POPOLO DI S. LORENZO

VIA DELLA STVFA

GERINI

BANDINELLI

SS.

SIGNORI

VIA DE GINORI

SCALA DI BRACCIA A PANNO FIORE

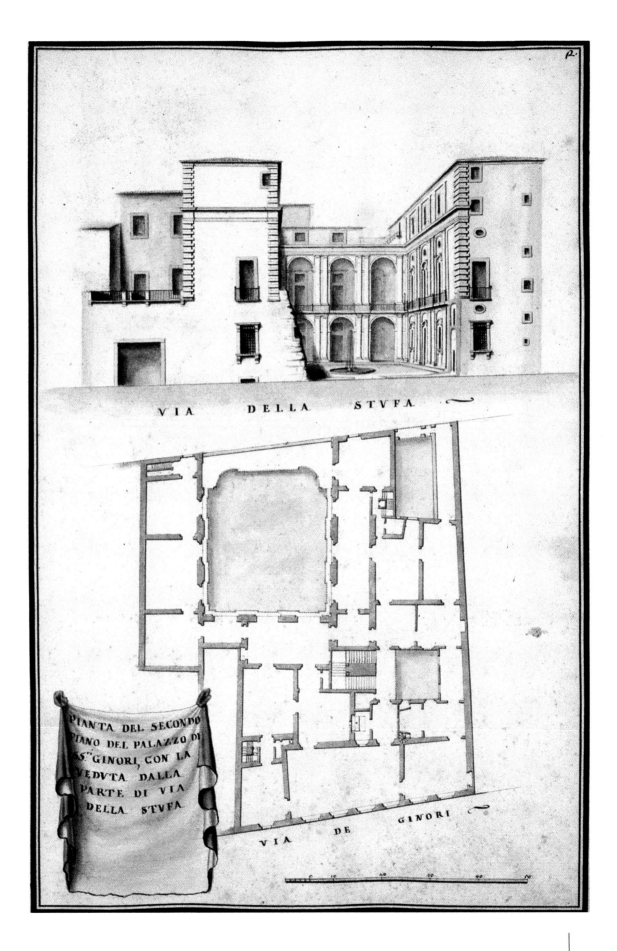

VIA DELLA STVFA

PIANTA DEL SECONDO
PIANO DEL PALAZZO DI
SS.ri GINORI, CON LA
VEDVTA DALLA
PARTE DI VIA
DELLA STVFA

VIA DE GINORI

PALAZZO BUDINI GATTAI

a city garden of exotic plants and flowers

The large garden at Palazzo Grifoni was originally designed by Buontalenti, who worked on the Boboli garden. Now the property of the Budini-Gattai family, it is rich with flowering plants, shrubs, and trees, including palm, camellia, oleander, laurel, box, and azalea.

Overleaf: *Jasmine vines, roses, irises, geraniums, and orange and banana trees thrive side by side. A lavender hedge, a laurel hedge, a chicory bush, and two southern magnolias frame the setting for a dramatic rock grotto at the far end of the garden. The pink azalea is a sure sign of spring.*

P alazzo Grifoni, now Budini Gattai, was built for Ugolino di Iacopo Grifoni by the architect Barto-lommeo Ammannati. Grifoni—first the majordomo to Duke Alessandro, and then secretary to Cosimo I—became rich and influential through his illustrious connections. Wanting a house befitting his station, Grifoni turned to Ammannati, who, along with Vasari, introduced the Mannerist style of Florentine architecture. A pupil of Michelangelo, Ammannati was one of the most innovative architects of the day. Palazzo Grifoni is considered a "most perfect example" of Ammannati's work.

The main part of Palazzo Grifoni was completed about 1574. Instead of the usual center courtyard, at the back of the house is a large loggia with five arches opening into a spacious garden. It is thought that the construction of the fountain in the garden may have involved Ulrico Middeldorf, and the figure of Venus atop the fountain may be the work of Giovanni Bandini.

During the seventeenth and eighteenth centuries the Grifoni family continued to prosper. The façade of the palace facing the piazza was finished, and in 1732 there was a great marriage—a Grifoni to the beautiful and social Lisabetta Capponi. Society in the mid-eighteenth century was a demanding whirl of events. Following the custom, Lisabetta had several *cicisbei*—the English writer Horace Walpole was among them. A *cicisbeo* was a family friend approved as an escort for a lady of nobility by her husband. This very practical system allowed the wife to attend all the parties while the husband took care of things he considered more important.

In 1890 the palace was bought by Cavalier Leopoldo Gattai and his son-in-law Francesco Budini. It was under their guidance that the palace was restored. Professor Giuseppe Boccini redesigned the interior in turn-of-the-century style. Today the impressive structure shelters a colorful and voluptuous garden, most surprising because of its generous size and wide variety of attractive plant life.

69

PALAZZO PANDOLFINI
the great art of Raphael in architecture

Early in the sixteenth century, Giannozzo Pandolfini, the Bishop of Troia, built a large and handsome house away from the city. He was one of several Florentines who wanted more light and space, and more land for extensive gardens. In his book, *The Palazzi of Florence,* Leonardo Ginori Lisci writes about these residences that carried the city to new limits: "Although these houses were still called palazzi in the mid-16th century, the gentlemen's residences later called Casini or lodges were certainly inspired by them. . . . Their huge gardens for both flowers and vegetables were almost more important than the houses themselves, and the owners derived amusement from the new hobby of cultivating decorative plants and rare fruits. Ponds, grottoes and leaping fountains proliferated, giving pleasure to the eye and serenity to the soul, so that the delights of country life could be enjoyed without the inconvenience of being cut off from the city."

Bishop Giannozzo Pandolfini was a friend of Pope Leo X (Giovanni de' Medici), and it was he who made it possible for the palace to be built by deconsecrating an oratory, allowing the property to be sold to Pandolfini. His gratitude is recorded on a frieze around the building. The palace was designed for Pandolfini by Raphael. Much of its early form remains, including an open loggia facing the garden. Through the centuries Palazzo Pandolfini has been a favorite of architectural historians, and accepted as the only house in Tuscany designed by the painter.

In the mid-nineteenth century the adopted nephew of Eleonora Pandolfini married Sofronia Stibbert, sister of the Scotsman Frederick Stibbert whose house is now a museum in Florence. The Pandolfini garden, one of the most important in the city when first conceived, again became much admired for rare botanical species. Countess Sofronia cultivated prize-winning camellias, and raised rare varieties of cineraria.

This historic building and spacious garden continues as the family seat of the distinguished Pandolfini family.

Palazzo Pandolfini, designed by Raphael in the early sixteenth century, has a surprisingly large garden. Figures from mythology line the entrance, leading to shaded paths that plumb the depths of the property. A variety of flowering plants are scattered throughout the garden, including day lily and rose borders in front of the laurel hedges.

At Palazzo Pandolfini, roses, fuchsias, and rhododendrons decorate the neoclassical pedestals that hold fanciful, mythological figures: Diana with her hunting dog; Minerva with her shield; Juno with a peacock; Venus with an apple; and Ceres with cornucopia and wine.

PALAZZO PITTI, BOBOLI GARDEN

a spectacular garden theater for centuries

In 1740 the pit of the amphitheater in Boboli was turned into a small parterre garden. It is now very ornamental, with roses in small box hedges. The beds are punctuated with lavender and oleander. Ivy climbs the walls to create an edging at the top. The Artichoke Fountain by Francesco Susini, built circa 1640, is a splendid display of the water brought to Boboli.

Overleaf: Along the olive walks, spectacular glimpses of Palazzo Vecchio and other Renaissance landmarks are offered. Pruned and pruned, the trees have become gnarled green sculptures.

Second overleaf: A drawing by Lambertini of the amphitheater, designed by Giulio Parigi and his son, Alfonso. The first production presented here in 1637 celebrated the wedding of Ferdinando II and Vittoria della Rovere, and is said to have included an equestrian ballet.

Palazzo Pitti and the Boboli garden are where art and nature meet in the most expansive way. The palace, the largest in Florence, and the garden, slightly over a hundred acres, are in a theatrical setting that rivals any in the world. Still in the city, a few steps from the Arno, and with the natural backdrop of the green hills that enclose the valley, Pitti and Boboli combine the design formality of a town palace and garden with the scale of a country villa and its rolling landscape.

In his history of Florence, Machiavelli wrote that the house being built for Luca di Bonaccorso Pitti was "larger than any constructed by a private citizen." And, indeed, Pitti, wanting a grand expression of his wealth, planned a palace based on designs by the master of splendor, Brunelleschi. Construction started before the great architect's death in 1446. The impressive structure, the open piazza to the front of it, and the garden to the back, replaced houses once owned by the Bogoli, or Bogolini. (Some say the name of the garden, Boboli, is derived from this family name.)

The palace was sold in 1549 to the wife of Cosimo I, the very rich Duchessa Eleonora di Toledo, and it soon became one of the favorite houses of the reigning Medici. Eleonora bought additional land and commissioned the architect Il Tribolo to design a garden suitable for court entertainments and official galas. One of Cosimo's great achievements, the building of aqueducts to bring fresh water into Florence, made a garden planned on a grand scale possible. Water was brought from nearby hills to Boboli, routed to Palazzo Vecchio, the main residence of the Medici, and on to fountains throughout the city to be enjoyed by all Florentines.

The architect Ammannati worked on the palace and the garden in the 1560s, and the pleasing result of bringing the two together can be seen in the lunette painted in 1599 by Giusto Utens (see page 59). Two wings and a courtyard were added to the palace, and the garden design made use of the natural horseshoe indentation in the hillside. Symmetrical

groves of several varieties of trees patterned the slopes, and surrounded a meadow of grass set with a spectacular fountain by the sculptor Giambologna. The effect was one of pure theater with an almost totally green backdrop—a perfect stage for royal receptions and amusements.

Eleonora took great interest in the garden, commissioning figures, fountains, and a small grotto called the Grotticina, which was executed by the architect Davide Fortini. Records show that, in 1563, a thousand asparagus plants were introduced to the garden. About the same time saffron crocus and dwarf fruit trees were added, and orange trees were trellised along a path to the side of the palace.

After the death of the Grand Duke Cosimo I, his son, Francesco I, continued working on the garden with architect Buontalenti. It was Buontalenti who built the fascinating Grande Grotta. Construction began in 1583 and took some ten years. The complex of three rooms is rich with depictions of humans and animals in rocaille work modeled by Piero Mati, with frescoes painted by Bernardino Poccetti. Slaves sculpted by Michelangelo appeared to support this fantasy cavern. Water and real vegetation added to the illusion.

In the seventeenth century, Cosimo II and Ferdinando II carried on the embellishment of Boboli. The magnificent amphitheater was constructed under the guidance of Giulio Parigi and his son Alfonso. When Pietro Leopoldo di Lorena (1765–1792) ascended to the Tuscan throne he opened the garden to the public. While adding more splendor to the palace he made many changes in the garden to give it a grander eighteenth-century appearance. Statues were added, fountains were restored, and the woods, orchards, and flower gardens were revitalized. Architect Zanobi del Rosso built the Kaffeehaus in 1776. An Austrian head gardener, Leopoldo Prucker, created the pineapple garden, and cultivated other exotic plants such as orchids. More greenhouses and tepidariums were constructed.

In an 1841 catalogue of the garden's plants, thousands of flower varieties and more than five hundred fruit trees were listed. This was during the reign of Leopoldo II, who is said to have taken a special interest in violets. A decidedly English influence was most apparent.

The amphitheater in Boboli continues to be a setting for opera and other musical performances The garden, with its great expanse of greenness, splashing fountains, collection of statues, and centuries of architectural and artistic decorations, is a wonder for serious students of garden design and a delight for anyone who responds to the magic of a large garden touched by genius.

In Boboli garden, a glimpse of the belvedere and the amphitheater. A laurel hedge and an Italian cypress stand in the foreground.

Overleaf: The garden's famous laurel arbor offers the visitor shade and a sense of how nature bends to man's desire. The circa 1565–68 Fountain of Neptune is by Stoldo Lorenzi. The god of the sea stands on a rocky mass that seems to be supported by humanlike sea creatures. The Neptune basin serves as a water reservoir for the garden.

Second overleaf: The Grande Grotta, designed by architect Bernardo Buontalenti in the 1580s, captures nature in a fantasy setting. The shepherd tending his flock, in stucco and rock work, is by Piero Mati. The scene of exotic animals and figures was painted by Bernardino Poccetti.

PALAZZO DEGLI ORTI ORICELLARI

a spacious garden for a heroic figure

annina de' Medici, the sister of Lorenzo the Magnificent, first bought land in 1481 in the area of the present Palazzo degli Orti Oricellari. About 1489 her husband, Bernardo Rucellai, added to the property. "Orti" refers to the original state of the land—an expansive space devoted to vegetables and fruit trees. "Oricellari" is the family name, Rucellai, latinized. It is said that a member of the Rucellai family found a perennial herb, "Rusca" (oricella) that, when wet with urine, turned from yellow to violet. This produced a dye for wool that brought a fortune to the family.

A palace was built on the property early in the sixteenth century from designs by the architect Leon Battista Alberti. It soon became a gathering place for Renaissance poets and scholars, who wrote about the garden and its Greek and Roman statuary. In 1573, the much-admired Venetian beauty Bianca Cappello bought the Orti and enhanced the garden, setting the scene for elaborate outdoor fêtes. She became the Grand Duchess of Tuscany and the property came to the Medici family through her marriage.

In 1640 the Orti became the residence of Cardinal Giovan Carlo de' Medici, who added many rare plants and flowers to the garden. He commissioned the sculptor Antonio Novelli to create the statue of Polyphemus and several fountains to use the water brought to the garden from Palazzo Pitti. Water reservoirs were covered with a mound of stones to resemble a cave den for the mythological giant. The brick, stucco, and iron figure, thirty-two feet high, stood on an island in the middle of a large pool.

After 1670 the Orti belonged to the Ridolfi family and close relatives. Early in the nineteenth century, Giuseppe Stiozzi Ridolfi asked the architect Count Luigi de Cambray-Digny to create a romantic English garden. Late in the century the property was saved from destruction by Marchese Ippolito Venturi Ginori and his wife, a Rucellai. Orti Oricellari now houses the Cassa di Risparmio di Pisa bank.

PALAZZO FRESCOBALDI

a green garden between palace and church

The garden of Palazzo Frescobaldi is a beautiful link to the family church, Santo Spirito—providing private access for joyous occasions such as family weddings. The garden has also acted as an escape route for the Frescobaldi family during times of trouble.

In the thirteenth and fourteenth centuries the Frescobaldis were one of Florence's most important and energetic families, very active in government and the social life of the city. They bought "less expensive land" on the other side of the Arno, and this became the site of the family palace. In 1282, to reach the center of the city more quickly, they had a bridge built near their property—it was the first Ponte a Santa Trinita. And, to buy a place in paradise, the family commissioned Brunelleschi to design the splendid basilica Santo Spirito. The façade was consecrated in 1481. Marcello Jacorossi, in his book, *Introduction to Florence,* writes: "With Santo Spirito it is the finest example in Florence of the clarity and strength of the Greek classical spirit tempered by a purely Latin sense of measure." The church and its bell tower, which enclose two sides of the garden, give the setting a tremendous sense of Renaissance drama. Family archives reveal that in order "to have the convenience of hearing Mass in Santo Spirito without leaving the house," in 1712 they built a small connection between the palace and the basilica with a tribune opening above the family chapel.

There are fascinating stories of colorful family members and others who entered their gates. Dino Frescobaldi was a famous poet and friend of Dante. When Dante was expelled from Florence, Dino rescued the early papers of the *Divine Comedy* and was able to return them to the author. It is said that Martin Luther, while still an Augustinian friar, celebrated Mass in Santo Spirito on his way to Rome. Girolamo Frescobaldi (1583–1643) was a well-known composer. Dianora Salviati, the wife of Bartolommeo de' Frescobaldi, set a record of her own by giving birth to fifty-two children, never less than three at a time, sometimes four or five—

A decorative grotto stands like a heroic portal at the far end of the garden at Palazzo Frescobaldi—a baroque contrast to the tower of the Renaissance church, Santo Spirito, and the contemporary sculpture by Arnaldo Pomodoro.

eleven survived. Bronzino painted a full-length portrait of this celebrated woman in handsome seventeenth-century dress. Another Bartolommeo Frescobaldi, in the same century, gave a much-talked-about party in his country villa. It was a gala of naked people, called the Ball of the Angels. When Pope Clemente XI heard about it he excommunicated him. To be reinstated Bartolommeo walked to Rome and endowed forty churches. Elizabeth Barrett Browning and her husband, Robert, considered taking an apartment in the palace. In one of her letters, written in 1846, discussing their choice of Casa Guidi for their living quarters, she writes: "Robert leaned once to a ground floor in the Frescobaldi palace being bewitched by a garden full of camellias, and a little pond of gold and silver fish." Florence Nightingale lived next door and must have enjoyed her garden view.

Beginning as a simple plot of vegetables and flowers, and evolving into a more decorative space, the garden has always been of great interest to the family. Cavaliere Angiolo Frescobaldi (1810–1892), the Grand Ducal Minister to the last Kings of Naples, was also a distinguished botanist. Marchese Lamberto Frescobaldi (1892–1959) was President of the Cassa di Risparmio di Firenze and an excellent agriculturist.

The form and content of the garden has changed as the life and occupants of the palace have changed. In the seventeenth and eighteenth centuries water for a fountain and the flowers was collected from the roof of the church. In the nineteenth century the space was completely redesigned. In 1810, Angelo Frescobaldi, a close friend of Leopoldo II and responsible for the education of Grand Duke Ferdinando II, asked the architect Pucci for a new and more formal plan. Trees were replanted and statues added. The garden now, although simplified, retains much of its character as a refreshing green space in an area of ancient stone buildings.

Pan casts a spell on the garden at Palazzo Frescobaldi. Sitting on a wall covered with English ivy, he is surrounded with oleander, laurel, and barberry. An azalea in full bloom in the background gives the statue a crown of pink.

PALAZZO ANTINORI
the city garden that grew with time

The garden of Palazzo Antinori is a fine example of a Florentine garden in the center of the city that evolved as property was acquired by a well-to-do and influential family over a long period of time. In the fifteenth century the Boni, rich from banking enterprises, bought several houses on what is now Piazza Antinori. These were demolished and an impressive palace was constructed sometime between 1461 and 1469. It is in the style of, if not by, architect Guiliano da Maiano. This well-proportioned building features traditional Florentine stonework, arched windows that echo the arched entrance, and a roof extended to create an imposing overhang. Inside there is a colonnaded courtyard and, beyond, a garden that has expanded and become more refined through the centuries as land and other houses were bought that now enclose the area.

In 1475 the palace was purchased from the Boni by Lorenzo the Magnificent, who soon sold it to friends, the Martelli family. In 1506 the palace was bought from the Martellis by Niccolò di Tommaso Antinori. The Antinori family, who had been in Florence since the early thirteenth century, were bankers and silk merchants active in government. With a great sense of social responsibility, Niccolò, in his will dated 1520, suggested to his children that "they should not be scanty in bestowing alms," as alms "always bear fruit."

Niccolò's son, Senator Alessandro, bought several houses behind the palace so the family holdings filled an entire block, creating a garden space that was then much as it appears now. It is also thought that he laid out the garden. Although the façade of the palace on the garden side has undergone several renovations, the door leading into the garden, with its classical columns and pediment, some believe is the work of Baccio d'Agnolo.

Several generations of Antinoris have distinguished the family in business, service to the state, and scholarly pursuits. A number of brilliant marriages have brought more wealth and extended their social sphere. In the eighteenth

The social and business life of the Antinori family is centered in their thirteenth-century palace. Its garden has a casual, modern-day charm. Terra-cotta pots and boxes around the old stone doorway bloom profusely with a variety of geraniums and multicolored petunias.

century the luxurious interior of the palace and the garden were the setting for gala parties. One that is still discussed was given for the Prince and Princess Esterhazy of Galata, with a particularly glittering guest list of princes and state dignitaries. In the early nineteenth century, considered a "golden age" for Tuscany, Senator Vincenzo Antinori took an active part in the cultural life of the court of Leopoldo II, and acted as tutor to his young sons.

Recently a major renovation of Palazzo Antinori and its garden was undertaken by the family. Supervised by the architect Emilio Dori, the entire palace was restored, regaining much of its former beauty. Part of the main floor is now devoted to the presentation of Antinori wines, which are produced on the family's country estate and for over a hundred years have been celebrated products of Tuscany.

John Ruskin wrote about the fertile lands of Tuscany in a letter to his father dated May 3, 1845: "You cannot conceive what a divine country this is just now; the vines with their young leaves hang as if they were of thin beaten gold—everywhere—the bright green of the young corn sets off the grey purple of the olive hills, and the spring skies have been every one backgrounds of Fra Angelico."

The generous garden space at Palazzo Antinori, with its panels of grass, flowering vines, and miniature gardens of bright flowers in terra-cotta containers, is nature in the city at its best.

In the garden of Palazzo Antinori, recently redesigned by architect Emilio Dori, green vines climb the walls, creating a backdrop for a graceful stone figure and flowering plants. Geraniums, bergenia, petunias, azaleas, and roses are among the flowers grown in this sun-filled place—typical of the palace gardens in the center of the city.

PALAZZO MALENCHINI

a family garden on the banks of the Arno

Walking along the Arno toward Via de' Benci, one pauses at the handsome gate and colonnaded walls for a glimpse of the garden of Palazzo Malenchini. While passersby delight in the plantings through the columns, the family can enjoy the life on the river from a raised walkway that runs the length of the wall. A decorative iron stair swirls up from the garden, and a balcony offers access to the *piano nobile* of the palace.

The palace and garden stand on property assembled by the Alberti family, who came to the area in the thirteenth century. Following local custom, as the family expanded they bought adjoining houses and shops that often had their own flower and vegetable gardens. These establishments eventually became the site of the family palace. When Leon Battista Alberti died childless in 1836, he left his fortune to his nephew, Mori Ubaldini, who commissioned the architect Vittorio Bellini to redo the palace and garden. The garden colonnade on the Lungarno side was his design, and he added an "Ionic tepidarium," patterned after the warm room in a Roman bath. In 1849 the architect O. Rezzi was asked to redesign the façade. Inspired by Michelozzo and Maiano, he achieved a fifteenth-century appearance.

Marchese Luigi Malenchini bought the palace at the end of the nineteenth century and through the years it has been a center for the city's social life. One of the most memorable balls was held in 1938 for Princess Maria José, daughter of the King of Belgium. The garden was lighted with Venetian lamps. Ladies found platters of gifts to give to the gentlemen who invited them to dance the beautiful quadrilles that filled the starry night.

The flood of 1966 caused great damage, but under the guidance of Marchese Piero Malenchini and his sons— the fifth generation of Malenchinis in the palace—the magnificent interior and garden have been restored and are again receiving guests in the gracious Florentine manner.

A sizeable garden with an arresting architectural entrance is an inviting feature of Palazzo Malenchini. The raised walkway along the river, shaded by wisteria, southern magnolia, and laurel, is a delightful place to promenade.

Overleaf: The sheltered garden is a pleasant place for a rest or read, and is a spectacular setting for an outdoor party. The plantings include crape myrtle, climbing roses, azaleas, camellias, maple and linden trees.

PALAZZO GONDI
a series of colorful, terraced gardens in the sky

A most spectacular garden in the sky is on three levels at the top of the venerable Palazzo Gondi. Between Palazzo Vecchio, the Bargello, the Badia, and the Duomo Santa Maria del Fiore, and so close one can almost touch them, this terraced garden is an utter surprise. The scene is brightly colored from the rusticated stones and roof tiles of surrounding buildings, and from trellised vines and terra-cotta containers filled with seasonal flowers. These delightful roof gardens were recently created by the architect Emilio Dori when the owner, Marchese Amerigo Gondi, asked him to undertake a major renovation of the building.

Palazzo Gondi, one of the most admired of the Renaissance palaces in Florence, was designed by the renowned architect Sangallo, who was much in favor with Lorenzo the Magnificent. Giuliano di Leonardo Gondi, a respected Florentine merchant banker, was able to live in the palace—although not completely finished—for several years, until his death in 1501. It is thought construction began about 1489, or shortly after. A planned extension was not finished until the nineteenth century, when architect Giuseppe Poggi was asked to carry out the task. He added a new entrance and a seventh window to the upper two floors on the façade facing Piazza San Firenze, and an entirely new façade on Via dei Gondi. Poggi was able to duplicate the handsome rusticated ashlars—the hewn paving stones that pattern the façades of the Renaissance palaces in Florence. The building is greatly appreciated for its strength and symmetry, and particularly for its interior courtyard with elegant columns and arches, and an open staircase, unusual in a courtyard, that is considered a Sangallo masterpiece. In 1652 the family was granted permission to use water from the fountain in the piazza and installed in their courtyard a beautifully carved fountain fashioned in several tiers. Later in the century some improvements were made from designs by architect Antonio Ferri. Splendid paintings, frescoes, and stuccowork were added.

Three rooftop terraces at Palazzo Gondi, situated between Palazzo Vecchio, the Bargello, the Badia, and the Duomo Santa Maria del Fiore, offer spectacular views of the tops of these Florentine landmarks. The brilliant colors of the potted geraniums, petunias, and oleanders enliven the scene enriched by the architecture of the surrounding buildings.

While the three penthouse terraces to the back of the palace catch the sun, supporting a variety of vines, shrubs, and flowers, the old *loggetta* on the roof to the front of the building offers shade. When shutters that protect an arched window to one side are opened there is the most astonishing view of the dome of the Duomo. It makes one acutely aware of Michelangelo's unfinished arcade around the dome. When only partially completed, Michelangelo had its construction stopped, deciding it was too fancy and made the dome look like a birdcage.

The flowers that bloom so extravagantly in and around Florence inspired D.H. Lawrence to write an essay called "Flowery Tuscany," dated about 1926–1927: "Tuscany is especially flowery. . . . it is the work of many many centuries. It is the gentle sensitive sculpture of all the landscape. And it is the achieving of the peculiar Italian beauty which is so exquisitely natural, because, man feeling his way sensitively to the fruitfulness of the earth, has moulded the earth to his necessity without violating it. . . .

"Yet Spring returns, and on the terrace lips, and in the stony nooks between terraces, up rises the aconites, the crocuses, the narcissus and the aspholed, the inextinguishable wild tulips. There they are, forever hanging on the precarious brink of an existence, but forever triumphant, never losing their footing."

In a letter to Dorothy Brett, dated July 7, 1926, Lawrence wrote: "Here it is full summer: hot, quiet, the cicadas sing all day long like so many little sewing machines in the leafy trees. The peasant girls and men are all cutting the wheat, with sickles, among the olive trees, and binding it into small, long sheaves. In some places they have already made the wheat stacks, and I hear the thresher away at a big farm. Fruit is in: big apricots, great big figs that they call fiori, peaches, plums, the first sweet little pears."

Geraniums, petunias, and variegated-leaf euonymus brighten the entrance to the loggetta on the rooftop of Palazzo Gondi. In the background: the Serragli family coat of arms on the Tribunale across Piazza San Firenze and the impressive façade and tower of the church of Santa Croce.

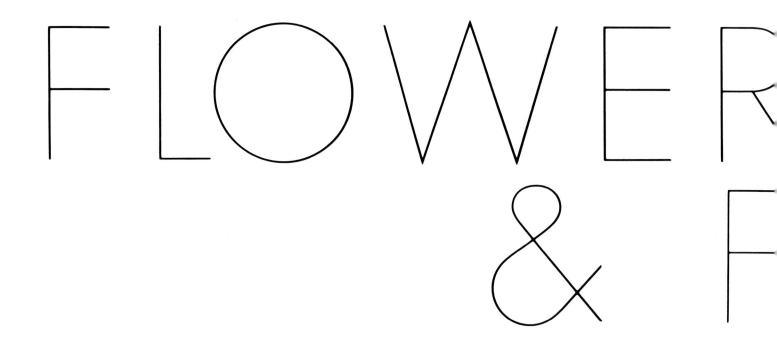

S
OLIAGE

Iris field at Villa La Limonaia.

THE VALLEY AND HILLS OF FLORENCE

a spectacular setting for the ideal garden

Certainly the favorable position of Florence on the world map contributes to the lushness of its vegetation, and perhaps to its life and art as well. The semitropical atmosphere of the city is enhanced by the shelter of the surrounding hills. Cloisters, atriums, and loggias in the palaces and villas create protected enclosures where plants thrive. Many terraced hillside gardens are designed with walls of stone, shrubs, or trees to shield them from the winds that sweep across the valley.

Plants from the tropics and trees from the north are at home in the valley of the Arno. The enormous variety of plant life is exciting. Studies of various archives have produced impressive lists of vegetation dating from Roman times. (The fact that marigolds and pansies bloomed for the Romans leads one to have more respect for these simple annuals.)

All of nature seems to speak Italian. Around Florence the greens are greener, the colors more vibrant, the scents sweeter than almost anywhere else. It may be because the gardeners use nature lavishly. Colors are massed together with a sense of extravagance. The flower beds are fuller, the flowering borders wider, the pergolas are encrusted with vines, and the arbors are voluptuous with climbing roses. Miniature gardens and orchards in the terra-cotta containers Florence is famous for are everywhere. Even the parterres are apt to be baroque.

Florence is called the city of lilies. The fleur-de-lis, the symbol of French kings, and the Florentine lily are the same design. It has been suggested that these lilies might well be irises. The lily, symbol of purity and the Virgin Mary, and the royal iris often appear in art and literature. Both flourish in the gardens and fields of Florence, adding color and fragrance to a land where nature responds so magnificently to the human hand and heart.

Brilliantly colored cineraria are planted in a bed bordered by boxwood. Vines, including grape, cover nearby arbors and make this part of the luxurious garden at Torre di Bellosguardo very green and inviting.

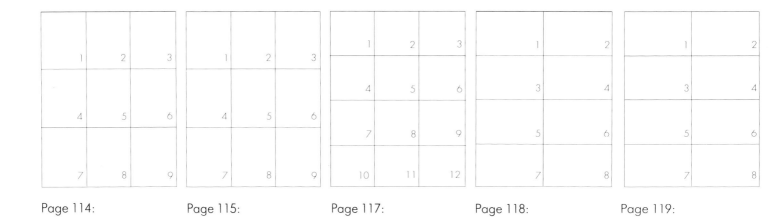

Page 114:

Page 115:

Page 117:

Page 118:

Page 119:

---

1. An allée of trees, vines, and azaleas, carpeted with wild flowers at La Gamberaia.
2. A venerable rose bush, said to be 150 years old, climbs the stairs in the Torrigiani garden.
3. Two heroic figures are the focus of a spacious parterre at Villa Torrigiani.
4. Roses, in a most sumptuous fashion, lead to another part of the garden at Torre di Bellosguardo.
5. A shaded, vine-covered pergola in the garden of Villa La Limonaia.
6. At La Limonaia, peonies and pansies are planted in the decorative terra-cotta pots Florence is famous for.
7. The parterre at Villa Capponi is enlivened with pink Silene pendula.
8. Sarabande roses and floribunda hedge roses at the German Institute.
9. An assortment of flowering plants and a spectacular view of Palazzo Vecchio from the Gondi terrace.

1. Roses flourish in the parterre garden at La Limonaia.
2. A room with a view of the formal garden at Villa La Limonaia.
3. Pots of calla lilies at Villa I Tatti.
4. Roses climb around a stone figure near the tower at Villa Torrigiani.
5. The dramatic path to the terraced garden at Villa Medici, Fiesole.
6. Clipped hedges and rosebushes create a romantic setting for stone figures at Villa La Pietra.
7. Stone figures, umbrella pines, and cypresses at Villa La Pietra.
8. A charming terra-cotta figure in a shell grotto at Villa La Gamberaia.
9. Flower beds and potted plants in bloom in the grotto at La Gamberaia.

1. Exotic birds-of-paradise thrive in the garden at I Tatti.
2. A vine-covered wall at I Tatti.
3. Cineraria at Villa La Limonaia.
4. Arbors, a pergola of roses, and a banana tree at Villa La Limonaia.
5. The parterre of lemon trees at Villa La Limonaia.
6. Campsis and leucojum at I Tatti.
7. Old English ivy at I Tatti.
8. Roses and lemons, cypress and southern magnolia at Villa Marchi.
9. Ivy, azaleas, and pansies at Villa La Gamberaia.
10. Roses and geraniums at the Convento di San Domenico.
11. Roses on the wall at Villa La Gamberaia.
12. Geraniums, southern magnolia, and cypress at Villa Marchi.

1. Roses and dictamnus at Villa La Limonaia.
2. Iris and cypress—favorites at Villa Limonaia.
3. An allée of holly at I Tatti.
4. Marigolds and clipped boxwood, Villa Capponi.
5. Roses bordered in box and yew at Villa La Limonaia.
6. Boxwood, laurel, olive, and cypress trees at I Tatti.
7. Roses and irises at Villa Torrigiani.
8. The holly-shaded drive at Villa Medici.

1. Cone-shaped dwarf conifers, boxwood beds, and climbing roses at Villa Torrigiani.
2. Rhododendron, boxwood, southern magnolia, cypress, and pansies at Villa La Limonaia.
3. Clipped yew and beds of marigolds at Villa Capponi.
4. Water lilies, climbing roses, and marigolds in boxwood beds at Villa Capponi.
5. Vines and bushes running wild surround two neoclassical statues at Museo Stibbert.
6. Irises and roses border a path at Villa La Limonaia.
7. A green setting for a stone figure at Villa Torrigiani.
8. Clipped yew and boxwood are part of the architectural setting in the garden at La Pietra.

ROMAN

M

TIC
ODERN

Egyptian folly at Villa Stibbert.

VILLA TORRIGIANI
a romantic nineteenth-century garden

The garden at Villa Torrigiani is one of the largest and most romantic gardens in the city. A series of paths lead to the villa, shaded by mature trees such as hackberry and horse chestnut.

Overleaf: *From the Torrigiani tower, there is a superb view. The tower is approached on one side along a grassy carpet strewn with wildflowers; on the other side, the tower is supported by the old city walls. Blue Atlas cedar, pine, juniper, yew, magnolia, ilex, linden, California cypress, and redwood trees are part of the landscape.*

Second overleaf: *A drawing of the garden from the mid-nineteenth century.*

Third overleaf: *The garden panorama includes statuary and plantings, such as rhododendron, laurel, cypress, cedar, juniper, aloe, and climbing roses. The stone figures and terra-cotta helmets on the gate are examples of the classical nineteenth-century style.*

When Raffaello Torrigiani bought property in Via del Campuccio in 1531, it was definitely away from the hub of the city. The two small houses there were converted to a large residence which was referred to as Casino del Campuccio. The land was particularly fertile. Numerous varieties of vegetables, fruits, and flowers were cultivated. An inventory records "groves of citrus fruit, trellises covered with Arabian and Catalonian jasmine, and hundreds of lemon and orange trees in pots." All of this was shown to guests at evening parties when the garden was illuminated with lamps. The famous botanist Pier Antonio Micheli, who worked in the garden from 1716 to 1718, is remembered with a monument.

In 1777 Cardinal Luigi Torrigiani died and left his estate to his great-nephew, Pietro, who took the Torrigiani name. The young, well-educated marchese envisioned a large, beautiful garden, and managed to assemble some twenty-five acres, including part of the old walls of Florence built by Cosimo I. Working with two architects, Count Luigi de Cambray-Digny and Gaetano Baccani, he created a most luxurious and romantic garden in the English style. In addition to a large parterre circled with a riding track, there were aviaries, hothouses, a temple, a grotto, and a number of follies. The focus of the garden was a tower that was set on a hill contained in the old city wall. Inspired by the Torrigiani coat of arms, the tower was symbolic, ornamental, and practical, as it offered a spectacular view of Florence.

The garden became known for its rare, prize-winning plants, attracting botanists and horticulturists from all over the world. It was, indeed, a nineteenth-century *giardino romantico*—a stage for outdoor life, including masked parties that were so fashionable at the time. The Torrigiani family continues to enjoy the shaded, winding paths, the velvety greenness of the rolling lawns, and the beauty of the classical sculptures—all a legacy of the garden's golden moment in the last century.

123

CIMITERO DEGLI INGLESI

a garden of stones, cedar and cypress trees

The English cemetery, or Cimitero degli Inglesi, is a much-visited garden of ancient stones and cypresses near the Porta a Pinti within the old walls of Florence. Admirers of Elizabeth Barrett Browning seek it out to marvel at her tomb there. A guidebook tells about this small Protestant oasis that dates from the early nineteenth century. Included are short biographies of some of the more well-known permanent guests. Their resting places are marked by carved figures and symbols of their pursuits in the style typical of the last century. It is recent history that has a certain charm.

Elizabeth and her husband, Robert Browning, loved Florence. She wrote often of her passion for the sun and the art of the city. The heady, romantic atmosphere inspired many of her greatest poems. The Browning's son, Pen, was born in Florence. Even their adored spaniel, Flush, thrived there. Elizabeth wrote in one of her letters: "Flush likes civilized life, and the society of little dogs with turned-up tails, such as Florence abounds with." She also mentions that Flush's noisy barking was "his way of speaking Italian."

In his book, *The Brownings of Casa Guidi,* Edward C. McAleer describes their apartment's rooms and terrace, enriched with comments from Browning letters: "In the spring of 1847, the terrace was 'green with quite high trees—daturas & others,' and the smell of lemon blossoms came through the open windows. That same autumn, the datura trees were covered with 'great white lilies, almost like the Victoria lily,' and the lemon tree had two ripening lemons. As the poets walked arm in arm on the terrace, they enjoyed the music of the choir and organ of the Church of San Felice across the street. By looking 'sideways' from the terrace, they could see 'the least tip of the Boboli trees against the sky.'"

The English cemetery, considered to be a museum of a certain portion of the city's history, is a small enclave of sculpted stones that tell vivid tales of some of the expatriates who have chosen Florence as their own.

Overleaf: *Mature cedars and cypresses shade the paths. The tomb of Elizabeth Barrett Browning is surrounded by marble dust from a recent restoration. In 1861 Robert Browning asked artist Frederick Leighton to design a monument for Elizabeth's tomb, which was patterned after the tomb of a Medici.*

ICI REPOSE
BON AUGUSTE DE MANNERHEIM
NÉ EN FINLANDE L'AN 1805
FLORENCE A SAN DONATO VILLA DEMIDOFF
LE 19 AVRIL 1879
AIMÉ ET REGRETTÉ

VILLA ANNALENA

a dramatic garden contoured for sun and shade

I n the mid-fifteenth century the Convent of Annalena was founded by Annalena Malatesta when her husband, Baccio d'Anghiari, a captain in the army, was killed in Palazzo Vecchio. The cloister has been replaced by a villa and the vegetable garden of the convent is now a picturesque garden of manicured hedges and mature trees. Situated between the Boboli and Torrigiani gardens, the property encompasses ramparts built by Cosimo I in 1530 as a bastion against Siena.

The present villa was constructed for Tommaso Corsi early in the nineteenth century, and the garden is sometimes still referred to as the Giardino Corsi. In 1819 Ferdinando III gave permission for water to be diverted from Boboli to the Corsi garden, which was designed by the well-known architect Giuseppe Manetti. The shape of the land inspired Manetti. On the Via Serragli side, the ground, held in by strong walls, is high above the roadway, a result of the walls built by Cosimo I. From this height the hill slopes down to a level where Manetti established a scrolled parterre, then rises again as it approaches the boundaries of Boboli. The contours of the earth allowed Manetti to create winding paths that rise and fall, twist and turn, bordered by a variety of shade trees. The effect is one of a much larger garden. The walks are enlivened with a sparkling fountain, trimmed hedges, stone figures, and a striking garden seat at the far end of the property which is decorated with a motif from the villa's façade.

During World War II the undulating earth was found to hold more than the old city walls of Cosimo I and the water conduits from Boboli. When it became necessary to dig a bomb shelter a series of military tunnels from Palazzo Pitti to the Arno were found. A part of Florence's history was uncovered in the garden.

Nathaniel and Sophie Hawthorne spent time in Florence in the first half of the nineteenth century, and stayed in the neighborhood of Villa Annalena. Sophie wrote: "The

Brilliant pink azaleas and very green laurel hedges are rich contrasts to the façade of Annalena, painted with the ochre color so favored in Florence. The garland trim gives the house a special architectural grace.

135

Lungarno was lighted with gas along its whole extent, making the cornice of glittering gems, converging in the distance, and the reflection of the illuminated border below made a fairy show. . . . Florence is as enchanting as I expected. It is a place to live and be happy in—so cheerful, so full of art, *so well paved.* It is delicious weather today, and the air is full of the songs of birds. The merlins are in choir over against our terrace, in a wood of the Torrigiani gardens. The marble busts, on their pedestals, seem to enjoy themselves in the bosky shade. The green lizards run across the parapet, and to exist is a joy. . . . Mr. Hawthorne is luxuriating down in the garden, buried up in roses and jessamine." Hawthorne wrote: "I hardly think there can be a place in the world where life is more delicious for its own simple sake than here."

Kate Field wrote about an evening in the garden at Villino Trollope in an article, "English Authors in Florence," published in *Atlantic Monthly*, December 1864. It captures the mood of gardens of that time that were designed for entertaining: ". . . in spring, when the soft winds kiss the budding foliage and warm it into bloom, the beautiful terrace of Villino Trollope is transformed into a reception room. Opening upon a garden, with its lofty pillars, its tessellated marble floor, its walls inlaid with terra-cotta, bas-reliefs, inscriptions and coats of arms, with here and there a niche devoted to some antique Madonna. . . . And here of a summer's night, burning no other light than the stars, and sipping iced lemonade, one of the specialities of the place, the intimates of Villino Trollope sit and talk of Italy's future, the last mot from Paris, and the last allocution at Rome."

Annalena's garden is larger than one would imagine at first glance. Pebbled paths lead through two parterres and, as the ground rises and falls, interesting areas of sun and shade are created. Old oak trees, trimmed boxwood, lacy Virginia creeper, and English ivy add to the green filigree patterns.

Overleaf: *At the far end of the garden, a seat decorated with garlands, which are seen on the façade of the villa, waits to be enjoyed. The greenery around it includes rhododendron and laurel. The swirling parterre is protected by ancient trees such as cedar and southern magnolia.*

MUSEO
STIBBERT

a wild garden of follies and fabulous trees

Now mostly wild, the garden at Museo Stibbert still shows vestiges of a glorious past. A tangle of Italian and English garden ideas, the vast acreage is still a pleasant place for walks and musings about its grander days. Classical statues, follies, and temples mingle with nature on the move. Vines are rampant, ancient trees untrimmed, shrubs and bushes reach in every direction, flowers bloom where the winds have taken them. The effect is romantic and rather mysterious.

The villa that houses the museum and the large garden were created by Frederick Stibbert, a Scottish officer who settled in Florence about 1860. He began to buy Italian paintings and decorative arts, and assembled an amazing collection of armor. The garden benefited from his eye for the unusual and was a delightful place to receive guests. Stibbert's sister Sofronia married the Count Alessio Pandolfini and lived at Palazzo Pandolfini on Via San Gallo. According to Leonardo Ginori Lisci the Countess "had a much admired collection of camellias in the historic garden of the palazzo and various rare species of cineraria in her winter garden."

In 1906 Stibbert gave his collections and property to the city of Florence to be used as a museum. The Pandolfini family is still involved in the museum's direction.

Susan and Joanna Horner describe their visit to Villa Stibbert in *Walks in Florence,* published in two volumes in London in 1873: "A lane to the right, winding up a short but steep ascent, leads to the Villa Stibbert. All the undulating land between the Via Vittorio Emanuele and the Via Bolognese bears the name of Mont'Ughi, from a certain Captain Ugo, who left Rome some time in the twelfth century in quest of adventures, or to make his fortune. Arriving with his band of armed followers in the vicinity of Florence, he wasted the whole country, and, finally, established himself on this height, where he built his castle, and where in modern days, an English gentleman, Mr. Stibbert, has converted two farmhouses into a beautiful villa. The story of Ugo is preserved in a fresco beneath a Loggia adjoining the house, painted by the Florentine artist Bianchi. From this Loggia a beautiful view may be obtained of hill and valley richly cultivated, which once was devastated by the robber chieftain. The little chapel beside the Loggia is supposed to occupy the site of Ugo's Castle, and within its walls lie buried the remains of the celebrated engraver Raffaelle Morghen, who died in 1833. . . .

"The grounds round the Villa Stibbert combine English taste for order with the usual elegance of the Italian garden, consisting of terraces decorated with lovely busts amidst the luxuriant growth of a southern vegetation. Within the villa there is a most rare and remarkable collection of armour, which Mr. Stibbert allows to be seen on certain days to those who can obtain a card of admission through his personal friends."

Like Stibbert, the English author Walter Savage Landor made Florence his home. Quoting from J. Forster's book, *Walter Savage Landor,* published in London in 1869, Landor's sentiments were these: "I have the best water, the best air and the best oil in the world. My country now is Italy, where I have a residence for life, and literally may sit under my own vine and my own fig-tree. I have some myrtles, pomegranates, gaggias, and mimosas in great quantity. I intend to make a garden."

In *The Golden Ring,* Giuliana Artom-Treves writes: "Flowers, like all things delicate and spontaneous, roused a protective tenderness in Landor. He was so fond of them that he would not let them by picked. For trees he had something akin to veneration."

Landor himself wrote in *Imaginary Conversations,* published in London in 1828: "Old trees in their living state are the only things that money cannot command. Rivers leave their beds, run into cities, and traverse mountains for it: obelisks and arches, palaces and temples, amphitheatres and pyramids, rise up like exhalations at its bidding; even the free spirit of Man, the only thing great on earth, crouches and cowers in its presence. . . . It passes away and vanishes before venerable trees."

Frederick Stibbert must have shared some of Landor's great feeling for trees. Along with working on the fourteenth-century-style villa for over half a century, Stibbert continued to add the trees and architectural elements that gave his garden its romantic character. Cypress of different species, varieties of pine, cedar, cork, Judas tree, red oak, white poplar, and black walnut are among the trees that stand as tributes.

Wild plants of all sorts grow in a small meadow at Museo Stibbert. The clearing is bordered by a row of lindens and cedars. A neoclassical-style figure stands in splendor, as does a very tall, heroic cypress.

Overleaf: A colorful garden temple is home to a romantic nineteenth-century stone figure. It sits in a tangle of plants and trees including palm, laurel, and oak.

VILLA LA PIETRA
an Englishman's garden in a style true to Tuscany

One of the most romantic gardens in the Florentine hills is at Villa La Pietra, where the roses seem to bloom more sweetly, and the hedges and lawns are the greenest of green. It is rare that the fortunes of war and the passing of centuries allow a Tuscan villa to stay in private hands. La Pietra has been blessed in this way, descending from one caring family to another. The present owner, Sir Harold Acton, tells of the villa's history and his life there in several of his books, including *The Villas of Tuscany,* and *Memoirs of an Aesthete.* His father and mother, Arthur and Hortense Acton, bought La Pietra at the turn of the century, and are responsible for the tasteful modernization of the villa. For Arthur Acton the rejuvenation of the seventeenth-century garden, enhancing and expanding it, became a passion.

There is a drawing in the Uffizi Gallery of how La Pietra looked in the fifteenth century. The name came from a stone pillar that marked the distance of one mile from the city gate of San Gallo where the villa stands. Distinguished families have owned the property—the Macinghi in the fourteenth century, the Sassetti family in the fifteenth. It was Francesco di Tommaso Sassetti, Sir Harold wrote, "who remodelled the villa in Renaissance style, married twice into the Strozzi and Pazzi families, and by his second wife he became the father of Francesco, the financial genius of the family." Francesco handled the banking in France for Cosimo de' Medici and Lorenzo the Magnificent. After twenty-eight years he returned to La Pietra and to his scholarly pursuits. The Capponis acquired the estate in 1547 from Francesco's heirs and kept it in the family for the next three hundred years. It was Luigi Capponi, a cardinal of the church, who saw that the villa was rebuilt. Baroque elements were added to the façade but much of the fifteenth-century structure was retained, and remains intact today.

Sir Harold wrote about the garden as it is now: "The whole garden is essential green; other colours are episodic

Pink, yellow, and scarlet roses—climbers and hybrid teas—neoclassical figures, and urns decorate the entrance to Villa La Pietra.

Overleaf: *The* limonaia *at the side of the villa is enclosed by walls patterned with rocks and shells. Clipped boxwood edges the beds that contain large, garlanded terra-cotta pots of lemon trees and colorful seasonal plants such as pansies.*

and incidental. Sunlight and shade are as carefully distributed as the fountains, terraces and statues, and in no other private Florentine garden have I seen statues of such individual strength and grace, from the lone colossus of Orazio Marinali to the Venetian figures of Francesco Bonazza which have stepped on to the open air theatre as for one of Goldoni's comedies. The wings of this little theatre are of clipped yew, the globed footlights of box. The statues, collected by my father for decades, deserve a separate monograph. It is a garden for all seasons, independent of flowers."

And in his memoirs Acton wrote: "The original garden, laid out on a steep hill-side, was almost destroyed in the nineteenth century when so-called 'English gardens' were all the rage, and it is ironical that my father, an Englishman, should have restored and reconstructed it on pure Tuscan lines. The process of 'tuscanization' began just before my birth, and my father refined upon the traces of the former garden and its retaining walls, with all the creative ingenuity of a *Cinquecento* architect. Most visitors are unaware of this, so homogeneous is the total impression."

During childhood Harold and his brother, William, "spent a lot of time in the garden, the resources of which were interminable. . . . there was always some new corner to explore, a hackneyed phrase but I can find no apter. There was the *pomario,* or walled orchard, with a sprawling *Stanzone* at one end which served as the winter quarters of our oranges and lemons and smelt sweetly of their blossoms and of gardenia. The juiciest peaches clustered by the *rocaille* walls, haunted by emerald lizards, and California tomatoes hung heavily, softening reddening in the sun, which saturated this spot more than any other. In the warm water of the central fountain frogs forgot to leap into hiding under the flat lily leaves and stared upwards as if hypnotized while thirsty dragonflies flashed past for a quick sip and bloated goldfish mouthed at insects drunk with honeysuckle."

"In the green dusk a ragged bat or two zigzagged low with a shrill twitter, and glow-worms lit up aquarium depths of aromatic herbs. A sudden rush of ideas that seemed altogether new, a crystalline alacrity of mind, was fanned by the evening breeze: the mellow walls absorbed one's secrets and the marble busts smiled down benevolently. Perhaps one was drugged by the mint and rosemary and verbena which floated to the nostrils by the incense of so many dreaming flowers."

Ancient wisteria creates an enticing entrance at one side of Villa La Pietra. A bed of bright pansies and a luxurious, pink climbing rose add to the magic.

Overleaf: Graceful neoclassical figures and an imposing stone portal are positioned on a terraced stage, like the actors and scenery in a nineteenth-century play. The very dramatic green is the result of carefully tended boxwood parterres and clipped yew. Ground covers include English ivy. Pine trees create shade and an occasional climbing rose and a horse chestnut in bloom bring color to the setting.

Th

Grapevine umbrella at Villa La Limonaia.

VILLA MEDICI
a hillside garden with a great history

Clinging to the hills of Fiesole, the Villa Medici was built for Cosimo the Elder by architect Michelozzo shortly after Cosimo bought the property in 1458. With its refreshing rural aspects and commanding view of Florence, the villa became a favorite retreat for Lorenzo the Magnificent, a place where he received diplomats and scholars and wrote sonnets praised by his poet friends. He almost met his end in this beautiful setting. The Pazzi family planned to murder Lorenzo and his brother Giuliano at the dinner table on the night of April 25, 1478, but when Giuliano failed to join the party, the assassination was postponed until the next day at mass in the Duomo. Giuliano was killed, Lorenzo escaped, and the conspirators were dealt with dramatically, thrown from windows with ropes around their necks. It was a colorful time for Florence and the Medici, a time of great intrigues and masterful planning. It was a moment for building great dynasties, elegant palaces, and impressive formal gardens—all well worth reading about.

Villa Medici has passed through many hands and renovations, but still enjoys one of the most arresting views in the Fiesole hills. In 1911 the villa was purchased by Lady Sybil Cutting. Her daughter, Marchesa Iris Origo, in her book, *Images and Shadows,* describes with much affection her childhood there. She tells of her first visit to the villa with her mother: ". . . she took me for a drive up a long hill, first between high walls over which yellow banksia roses tumbled and a tangle of wisteria, then through olive-groves opening to an ever wider view; and finally down a long drive overshadowed by ilex trees to a terrace with two tall trees—paulownias—which had scattered on the lawn mauve flowers I had never seen before. At the end of the terrace stood a square house with a deep loggia, looking due west towards the sunset over the whole valley of the Arno. . . . This, then, until my marriage fourteen years later, became my home, and certainly no child could have had a more beautiful one."

On the terrace at the Villa Medici, now owned by the Marchi family, the formal garden is patterned with a small parterre and four southern magnolias pruned in striking cone shapes. A vine-covered pergola leads to the villa.

157

And, writing about her mother's care of the property: "She restored the Villa's formal garden to its original design and furnished the house from the Florentine *antiquari* . . . with the help of two gifted young architects, Geoffrey Scott and Cecil Pinsent, who were then working for the famous Bernard Berenson, at his villa at Settignano, I Tatti, and sometimes with the Olympian advice of B.B. himself."

About the garden, she writes: "Whenever I was free of my governesses, I escaped into the garden, not to the formal terrace, with its box-edged beds and fountains where my mother took her guests, but to the dark ilex wood above it or the steep terraces of the *podere,* partly cultivated with plots of wheat or of fragrant beans, partly abandoned to high grass and to the untended bushes of the tangled, half-wild little pink Tuscan roses, perpetually-flowering, *le rose d'ogni mese.* This became my domain."

The woods of Tuscany also beckoned writer D.H. Lawrence. In a letter to Martin Secker dated April 29, 1927, he wrote: "It's sunny weather, full summer, and very lovely weather, not a cloudy day these last twenty days. We have come to the lying in the garden stage, and I go off into the woods to work, where the nightingales have a very gay time singing at me. They are very inquisitive and come nearer to watch me turn a page."

In her book, *Pascarel,* published late in the last century, the romantic Ouida wrote: "Where lies the secret of the spell of Florence?—a spell that strengthens, and does not fade with time?

"It is a strange, sweet, subtle charm that makes those who love her at all love her with a passionate, close-clinging faith in her as the fairest thing that men have ever builded where she lies amidst her lily-whitened meadows."

At Villa Medici, the interior of a rock-encrusted pavilion is decorated with frescoes, including a trompe l'oeil view of the lanes that lead to the entrance gate and to the terraced garden below.

VILLA
FERRAGAMO
a garden of terraces
with magnificent
views

In hills of cypress high above Florence, Villa Ferragamo has a spectacular view of the city and the surrounding valley. Terraces are walled with green vines such as bougainvillea. Camellias flourish and geraniums in profusion spill out of giant terra-cotta jars and an old wellhead. The jars are almost like architectural elements, adding great drama to the pebbled terrace that runs the full length of the villa.

A perfect example of how the natural slope of a hillside can be terraced into a series of interesting gardens—each one with its own personality—can be seen at Villa Ferragamo in Fiesole. One garden leads to another, and then another, and then another, in the old Italian way. The villa is one of the handsome Renaissance-style structures admired for its sturdy construction and simplicity of line. It sits on a promontory of land that allows an extraordinarily wide view of the Arno valley. The orchards, vineyards, and open fields below are sprinkled with the red tile roofs of farmhouses and other villas. A front terrace, furnished with comfortable seats and colorful flowers, runs the full length of the house and takes advantage of the vista. Directly beneath it, another long terrace is ornamented with giant terra-cotta jars brimming with geraniums or lemon trees that are placed at random, like pieces of sculpture. To one side, and down some stairs, there is a spacious green lawn and the camellia bushes that produce prize-winning flowers for Mrs. Wanda Ferragamo, the villa's owner. There are other green areas as the land rises— paths for shaded walks, a grove of old trees that offers all the pleasures of a deep wood. Everywhere terrace walls are covered with flowering vines and lined with terra-cotta containers filled with flowers of the season.

A big garden that is really a series of small gardens is an idea the Italians have perfected through the centuries. The concept may have flourished simply because Italy is a country of dramatic hillsides, or perhaps because it is just the clever way Italian gardeners refresh the eye while exhibiting as many of nature's gifts as possible. Visiting an Italian garden that has been divided into a number of rooms, like an extension of the house, is a most delightful garden experience. Being surrounded by some of the world's great art and architecture in everyday life must certainly contribute to the Italian gardener's fine sense of composition, color, and texture so evident in these rooms in the garden.

Edith Wharton, who visited many villa gardens early in the twentieth century, wrote in *Italian Villas* that "a garden which is merely one huge outdoor room is also less interesting and less serviceable than one which has its logical divisions. Utility was doubtless not the only consideration which produced this careful portioning of the garden. Aesthetic impressions were considered, and the effect of passing from the sunny fruit-garden to the dense grove, thence to the wide-reaching view, and again to the sheltered privacy of the pleached walk or the mossy coolness of the grotto—all this was taken into account by a race of artists who studied the contrast of the aesthetic emotions as keenly as they did the juxtaposition of dark cypress and pale lemon-tree, of deep shade and level sunlight. But the real value of the old Italian garden-plan is that logic and beauty meet in it, as they should in all sound architectural work. Each quarter of the garden was placed where convenience required, and was made accessible from all the others by the most direct and rational means; and from this intelligent method of planning the most varying effects of unexpectedness and beauty were obtained."

Wharton wrote this about lawns: ". . . it must not be thought that the Italian gardeners did not appreciate the value of turf. They used it, but sparingly, knowing that it required great care and was not a characteristic of the soil. . . . These bits of sward were always used near the house, where their full value could be enjoyed, and were set like jewels in clipped hedges or statue-crowned walls. Though doubtless intended chiefly for games, they were certainly valued for their aesthetic effect, for in many Italian gardens steep grass alleys flanked by walls of beech or ilex are seen ascending a hillside to the temple or statue which forms the crowning ornament of the grounds." At Villa Ferragamo, the lawn is a refreshing green expanse among the garden's terraced rooms.

At Villa Ferragamo, the terrace walls are an important part of the greenery. In this semitropical climate, many plants native to northern and southern climates grow happily side by side. Pomegranate, camellia, fig vine, and iris are among the varieties that thrive here.

162

VILLA SAN MICHELE
a hilltop garden of beauty and luxury

High in the hills of Fiesole there is a small luxury hotel, Villa San Michele, that began as a Franciscan monastery dedicated to St. Michael the Archangel. The property, a farm with vineyards, woods, and a stream that gave the area the name of *alla Doccia,* was bought in 1411 by Niccolò Davanzati as a gift to the Franciscans. In addition to honoring St. Michael annually, the monks were to recognize the gift in various symbolic ways. One puzzling way was by giving their patron a pound of wax on St. Michael's day.

In 1596 Giovanni Davanzati undertook restoration of the building. Contracts show that Michele del Barba, a local stonecutter, carried out the work from plans by Santi di Tito. Tito's designs were influenced by Michelangelo—an interesting link between the great Renaissance artist, who grew up nearby, and his patron saint, to whom the monastery was dedicated. The monastery remained in church hands until Napoleon arrived to suppress the religious orders and confiscate their lands. After Grand Duke Ferdinand's return, Dr. Frosini-Martinussi bought the property and turned the building into apartments. He replaced a kitchen garden with a formal parterre. Some of the beauty of the monastery still existed when Henry White Cannon of New York acquired it in 1901. Repairs and some changes were made, and the garden was revived and improved.

Shortly after World War II the damaged villa was sensitively restored by M. and Mme. Lucien Teissier, who transformed it into a hotel of distinction. Now under the direction of the Hotel Cipriani of Venice, the present owner, and with the help of architect Gerard Gallet, the handsome villa has regained much of its original character. It is a place of comfort and luxury in the Cipriani tradition. The imposing arcaded entrance and the elegant loggia that runs all along one side, the poetic setting of the terraced gardens, and the splendid view of the valley make San Michele one of the jewels in Florence's crown of Renaissance villas.

On the entrance loggia of Villa San Michele, terracotta containers of seasonal flowers add to the warm welcome visitors receive at this historic place. May color is provided by azaleas, marguerites, and geraniums. The redesign of the façade during the sixteenth century was influenced by Michelangelo.

The surrounding hills are lush with villas and gardens, farms and fields. The scene in the late nineteenth century is described with much feeling by Marie Louise de la Ramée, who, under the name of Ouida, produced some forty-nine books. She settled in the hills of Florence and in her book, *Pascarel,* wrote: "The delights of an Italian garden are countless. It is not like any other garden in the world. It is at once more formal and more wild, at once greener with more abundant youth and venerable with more antique age. It holds Boccassio between its walls, all Petrarca in its leaves, all Raffaelle in its skies.

"The old broken marble statues, whence the water dripped and fed the water lily; the great lemon-trees in pots big enough to drown a boy, the golden globes among their emerald leaves; the magnolias, like trees cast in bronze. . . . high walls, vine-hung and topped by pines and cypresses; low walls with crowds of geraniums on the parapets, and the mountains and the fields beyond them; marble basins hidden in creepers where the frogs dozed all day long; sounds of chapel bells and of chapel chimes."

Olive Hamilton, who included this excerpt from *Pascarel* in *Paradise of Exiles,* said that "Ouida came to the land of Dante, where she was welcomed as a famous writer and, moreover, like Byron before her, a rich and eccentric one." About Ouida renting the villa Farinola, Hamilton wrote: "Since the English, unlike the Italians, always seem to this day to choose a house for its view rather than for its architecture or amenities, to someone like Ouida, who loved beauty in nature and romantic ruins, it must have seemed perfection, particularly as her garden was a formal Italian garden, with box hedges and lemons; and the lawns sloping from the terrace were limited only by a low stone wall beyond which the rounded hills clad in olive groves and vineyards stretched to the horizon."

Lord Byron wrote in *Childe Harold's Pilgrimage* about the Arno valley: "But Arno wins us to the fair white walls,
Where the Etrurian Athens claims and keeps
A softer feeling for her fairy halls.
Girt by her theatre of hills, she reaps
Her corn, and wine, and oil, and Plenty leaps
To laughing life, with her redundant horn.
Along the banks where smiling Arno sweeps
Was modern Luxury of Commerce born,
And buried Learning rose, redeem'd to a new morn."

The garden façade of Villa San Michele is covered with an ancient wisteria vine. During the month of May it blooms profusely and acts as a great backdrop for the rest of the garden. Decorative terra-cotta pots of lemon trees add further color. Above the villa are two terraced hillsides, lush and green with flowering plants and ground covers. From this garden there is an exhilarating view of the city and the hills beyond.

166

VILLA LA GAMBERAIA
the poetry of a water parterre in the garden

An intriguing pattern of pools reflects the intense greenness of the grand open garden at Villa La Gamberaia. At one end, like a stage set, is an arresting curved screen of trained topiary pierced with tall arches that open to a glorious view of the valley and the Apennine hills beyond. As it curves around a pool of water lilies, the screen draws the eye and gives it a most agreeable place to rest. Brilliant color from the occasional vibrant rose or other seasonal flower punctuates the greenness of the pruned yew, boxwood, and cypress that gives the garden its shape. Taking advantage of the terraced hillside, the rather limited acreage is divided into a series of gardens—the grand garden, the lemon garden, the grotto at the far end of the property that is approached by a long alley of green lawn, an almost-secret rock garden, a vegetable garden, a shaded wood. During the several hundred years of its existence, La Gamberaia has had its share of neglect and endured the ravages of war. It has been rescued several times—once, at the end of the last century by Princess Giovanna Ghyka, who restored the water parterre, and most recently by the Marchi family, who completely rebuilt the villa and garden after it was destroyed in World War II.

Everyone seems to agree that the villa was built early in the seventeenth century. An inscription has been found, dated 1610, indicating that this is when the house was completed for Zanobi Lapi. He died only nine years later, leaving the property to his two nephews. It remained in the family until about 1717, when the estate was divided between the Capponi and the Cerretani families. There is speculation about the origin of the name, Gamberaia, but it is possible that it is derived from the *gamberi,* or crayfish, that were caught in a spring-fed pool nearby. Another theory relates the name to the Gamberelli family, who lived in the neighboring village of Settignano. Their coat of arms includes six crayfish.

Securing sources of water for the garden is part of the

One of the rock grottoes at Villa La Gamberaia is decorated with fantasy figures surrounded by ancient cypresses. The large circular bed, filled with colorful verbena, is neatly enclosed by a clipped boxwood hedge.

villa's colorful history. Contracts dated between 1624 and 1635 show that Zanobi Lapi's nephew, Andrea, bought springs and the right to build reservoirs and channels to carry water to the pools and fountains in the villa garden. Janet Ross, in *Florentine Villas,* published in 1901, wrote that she found the remains of conduits and tanks, "to attest the considerable works made by Andrea Lapi for supplying water to his beloved villa. He no doubt planted the noble cypresses that tower like dark green steeples on either side of the long bowling alley that runs for some four hundred feet behind the house, ending to the north in one of the elaborate half grottoes, half fountains, inlaid with shells and decorated with stone figures of impossible animals and queer people in high relief. . . . To the south the long green walk ends in a delightful old stone balustrade with solemn grey figures, from whence the view over the fruitful, gently rolling hills crowned with villas or peasant houses is beautiful."

In *Italian Villas and their Gardens,* published in 1904, Edith Wharton wrote this about the garden at La Gamberaia: ". . . it combines in an astonishingly small space, yet without the least sense of overcrowding, almost every typical excellence of the old Italian garden: free circulation of sunlight and air about the house; abundance of water; easy access to dense shade; sheltered walks with different points of view; variety of effect produced by the skillful use of different levels; and, finally, breath and simplicity of composition."

Sir Harold Acton, who knows La Gamberaia well, wrote about the garden with much feeling in his book, *Great Houses of Italy,* published in 1973: "Were I asked which garden near Florence is the most poetical, I would answer without hesitation that of the Villa Gamberaia. . . . All of its previous owners must have loved the place, for its supreme quality is a serene harmony of liquid mirrors and rhythmical plants. . . . The Lapi family spared no expense to provide their garden with abundant water, enabling their successors, Antonio and Piero Capponi, to lay out the garden in sophisticated eighteenth-century style. Owing to this wise forethought, it has an air of perennial freshness. . . . The pools reflect such a feast of shimmering colour that the eye is dazzled. . . . It is a hall of horizontal mirrors terminating in a theatrical arcade of clipped cypresses. . . . Nowhere else in my recollection have the liquid and solid been blended with such refinement. . . . It leaves an enduring impression of serenity, dignity and blithe repose. All garden lovers are indebted to its present owner for healing its war wounds with such consummate art."

The famous ornamental garden at Villa La Gamberaia with its well-trained and -pruned topiaries of yew, boxwood, and cypress.

Overleaf: *A series of shallow pools reflect blue sky, green hedges, and an array of colorful flowers. A spectacular view of the valley below is framed by the screen of green at the far end of the garden.*

Second overleaf: *Views of the grand ornamental garden nearest the villa.*

VILLA I TATTI

a garden in Anglo-Florentine style

An allée of cypress trees leads to a stair of architectural intrigue. The stairway, covered and surrounded with green, swirls to an upper level. Terraces and architectural elements are important aspects of the garden at I Tatti.

In 1887 Bernard Berenson graduated from Harvard University and, with the help of his friend Isabella Stewart Gardner, sailed to Europe and a life immersed in the arts. By 1894 he was an established art authority guiding Mrs. Gardner and others in the formation of exceptional collections of Old Master paintings and Renaissance treasures. Unable to resist the beauty of the Tuscan hills around Florence, and sensing that it was an ideal setting for his work, in 1905 Berenson and his wife Mary bought I Tatti, a house they had rented for several years in Settignano. Berenson asked English architect Cecil Pinsent to reconstruct the building and design a garden. Between 1908 and 1915 evolved a most attractive, livable villa with an indoor garden and lemon house extended into a dramatic terraced garden with a splendid view of the valley below.

In *The Villas of Tuscany,* Harold Acton makes this comment about the garden: ". . . it has the Pinsent touch. In other words it is Anglo-Florentine; its Tuscan elements have been cleverly adapted rather than absorbed. The scale as well as the dainty precision of the details is more English than Florentine." This mixture of ideas gives the garden the special character that pleased and enriched Berenson's remaining forty-four years. In *Sketch for a Self-Portrait,* Berenson's passionate feeling for the garden is expressed in several passages that span the years of his life from age sixty on:

"Returning to the garden I had planted, by the time it had grown and could be enjoyed, hurry seized me; and for the arbours and fountain curbs where I was to sit and listen to the nightingales, blackbirds, thrushes and larks, and draw in the fragrance of roses, lotuses, and lime blossoms I never found the leisure. I could only glance and pass on.

"Long before I felt so indulgent and kindly to members of my own species I used to think that if I loved human beings as I loved trees I should be a saint. To this day the death of a noble cypress or mighty oak or tremulous poplar affects me more than all but few men and women whose necrology I read in the newspapers.

"The most gifted authors can seldom say anything satisfactory about a concrete object without singing it; I wish I could sing about flowers and colours. Each day I seem to appreciate both more. I look and say: 'What have my eyes been that I have not realized as I do this morning the spread of that rose, the turn of its petals, the exact shade of its varying reds or yellows or whites; or the translucency of the tissues in the rhododendron, azalea or morning glory.'

"I have a garden too, as I mentioned earlier. Unless it pours with rain I run through it at least once a day, to taste the air, to listen to the sound of birds and streams, to admire the flowers and trees. I wonder whether art has a higher function than to make us feel, appreciate and enjoy natural objects for their art value? So, as I walk in the garden, I look at the flowers and shrubs and trees and discover in them an exquisiteness of contour, a vitality of edge or a vigour of spring as well as an infinite variety of colour that no artifact I have seen in the last sixty years can rival. And beyond the garden, as I walk on the olive-crowned, pine-plumed, cypress-guarded hills, I enjoy the effect of clouds under the high and spacious dome of the sky, the hazes between me and the horizon— toward Siena, toward Volterra, toward Pisa, toward Carrara—hazes leaden on dull days, silvery in the winter, pearly in spring and autumn, and golden at midsummer. Each day, as I look, I wonder where my eyes were yesterday. Why did I not perceive the beauty of the lichen-trimmed tree-trunk as gorgeous as an Aztec or Maya mosaic; of that moss of a soft emerald that beds your eye as reposefully as the greens in a Giorgione or Bonifazio; and why had I been blind to the jewelled elaboration of the honey-suckle and to the enamelled elegance of the purplish black and ruby butterfly that flutters about those slopes? So, health permitting as happily as it still does, I do not need to roam nor even to soar; for every morning, every afternoon as I go out of doors, I discover more than enough newness to suffice for the day."

Cecil Beaton described a visit with Berenson at I Tatti in his book, *The Face of the World:* "Soon we were out of doors, walking under an avenue of pale lime trees in bud, while I took photographs of my venerable host in the course of the promenade. Berenson pointed out a walled garden above us, where the wisteria was already in bloom. We went down a steep incline to the meadows, and were soon in a paradise of spring wild flowers. Berenson observed that, after a lifetime of observation, he was only beginning to look at things—nature claimed his attention as much if not more than man's art. Each day brought some new insight into the

In the garden at Villa I Tatti there is a choice of stair leading from one terrace to another—a design element with much finesse. The niche between the two stairs is filled with potted calla lilies. The shape of this interesting garden structure is enhanced by a covering of English ivy.

shape of a hill or an olive tree; a crimson anemone in the grass stirred a perennially newborn vision; the blue of the sky reflected in a pool was ample cause for wonder. As he commented on the beauty around him, I was aware that, in his company, life took on an added intensity. Even the brief conversation we had already had seemed to have provoked a series of simple visual discoveries."

Like Berenson, writer Henry James loved the hills and villas of Tuscany. In *The Portrait of a Lady,* he describes a villa garden: ". . . the villa overhung the slope of its hill and the long valley of the Arno, hazy with Italian colour. It had a narrow garden, in the manner of a terrace, productive chiefly of tangles of wild roses and old stone benches, mossy and sun-warmed. The parapet of the terrace was just the height to lean upon, and beneath it the ground declined into the vagueness of olive-crops and vineyards."

James wrote of Isabel Archer's visit to Osmond's villa and tea on the terrace: "The sun had got low, the golden light took a deeper tone, and on the mountains and the plain that stretched beneath them the masses of purple shadow seemed to glow. . . . The scene had extraordinary charm. The air was almost solemnly still, and the large expanse of the landscape, with its gardenlike culture and nobleness of out-line, its teeming valley and delicately-fretted hills, its peculiar-ly human-looking touches of habitation, lay there in splendid harmony and classic grace."

Bernard Berenson, considered by many to be the "most celebrated humanist and art historian of our time," died in 1959. He bequeathed I Tatti to Harvard, which estab-lished it as an art study center. Hundreds of students have benefited from the villa's extensive library and pleasant sur-roundings, and the cultural riches in nearby Florence.

The beauty of the terraced garden at I Tatti is greatly heightened by its natural setting. Steps patterned with stones add interest to the shaped hedges that frame beds for seasonal plantings. Standing on the lower level, one is in a completely green enclosure with only the cypresses and umbrella pines reaching into the sky.

Overleaf: *The old, finely clipped boxwood parterre.*

VILLA
MARCHI
terrace views
framed by arches
of cypress

At Villa Marchi trained cypresses create walls for this small garden designed around a pond of water lilies. Southern magnolias contribute lacy shade.

Overleaf: As in most gardens in the Florentine hills there are terraces at Villa Marchi. Here, one terrace is designed as a winter and summer limonaia. The structure is decorated with stone designs. Above it is a pergola covered with wisteria.

The garden at Villa Marchi is a series of green rooms, terraced and enclosed in walls of cypress. These evergreen walls are pruned, shaped, and punctuated with tall arches that frame views of the valley of Ema that stretches for miles on either side. It is an architect's dream of a garden. Each terrace, contained and controlled, is treated separately. The cypress walls give the garden a great sense of style. Richard Blow, who bought the villa in 1926, is responsible for much of the current layout, and it is reported that he consulted the architect Cecil Pinsent, who designed the garden at I Tatti for Bernard Berenson.

Blow also made sensible alterations to the villa, which dates from a house called "La Costa" that was built in the early fifteenth century and belonged to a famous doctor, Cristofano di Giorgio Brandolini. Through the centuries the property changed hands—one distinguished family after another—until, at the end of the nineteenth century, it was owned by Don Francesco Paternò, Duke of Carcaci. It was he who eventually sold it to Richard Blow.

In the mid-seventeenth century, when the villa belonged to Caterina Landini, certain renovations were made that gave it a distinct seventeenth-century look—vestiges still remain. One enters, through the old main door, into a courtyard that is enclosed on three sides by wings of the house. The fourth side, to the south, is an open terrace that looks over the valley, and is an entrance to the garden that descends on several levels. The present owners, the Marchi family, also enjoy another entrance to the garden from the front of the villa. It crosses over the top of a *limonaia* terrace and a closed loggia that shelters the potted lemon trees in the winter. This glassed-in winter garden is a decorative and practical structure. The patterns of pebbles and stones are full of fantasy, entertaining the eye and contributing to the overall texture of the garden design.

CONVENTO DI SAN DOMENICO

a cloister garden where the rose is celebrated

Climbing roses—mostly in pinks, peaches, and yellows—frame the gate that opens into a colorful rose garden at the Convento di San Domenico in the Florentine hills.

Overleaf: *Facing loggias enclose this cloister garden. Roses, geraniums, bergenia, and laurel create a varied garden palette. Terracotta tubs, pots, and boxes are placed here and there to delight the eye. The walls of the old convent protect the garden from the winds, and pebbled paths bordering panels of grass make this a pleasant place for walks.*

There are small Chinese roses that flourish in the environs of Florence—the climber is apt to be a delicious yellow, and the shrub a delightful pink. These, along with many other varieties of roses, thrive in the cloister garden of the old Convento di San Domenico in the Arcetri hills. The convent, a private residence since the turn of the century, has an interesting history that dates from about 1269, when it was a place of contemplation for Augustinian monks. Around 1400 the convent became the home for the nuns of St. Clara and St. Francis.

By the early seventeenth century it had become the Convento di San Matteo, and two daughters of Galileo lived there. Galileo's own house and observatory were nearby. There is a story that Galileo's daughter by his wife was allowed to write to him, while his other daughter, by another woman, was not. In a letter dated December 19, 1625, Sister Maria Celeste wrote that she and Sister Arcangela sent him much affection and good wishes for his health and, along with the letter, included some citron and two baked pears she had prepared. Most importantly she sent him a late-blooming rose—a December rose from the cloister garden of the convent was a special gift. She explained that the thorns represented the passion of the Christ and the leaves signified hope, both reminders that the winter of this life would be followed by an eternal spring in heaven.

Even today the roses bloom late in this sheltered garden, tended with much care by the family that has owned the residence, still referred to as the Convento di San Domenico, for almost a hundred years.

VILLA CAPPONI
topiary parterres filled with lemon trees and flowers

A well-patterned parterre is the setting for the limonaia at Villa Capponi. Lemon trees in giant terra-cotta pots sit in beds of pink Silene pendula bordered by clipped boxwood hedges. Even the wall enclosing the garden is shaped: the unexpected, undulating top, decorated with urn finials, adds additional texture and design to the garden.

Overleaf: A lush, green lawn leads to the lemon garden; two terra-cotta griffins guard its entrance.

Second overleaf: The villa terrace looks into the old parterre garden over a wall of wisteria, climbing roses, and jasmine.

Third overleaf: The parterre of pink Silene pendula is bordered with boxwood topiary borders, and is contained within decorative vine-covered walls.

The old parterres at Villa Capponi are some of the most enchanting gardens near Florence. The terraces at this comfortable villa in Arcetri offer the most spectacular view of the Arno valley. Enclosed in scalloped walls trimmed with urn finials, the boxwood has been shaped into geometrical hedges topped with round topiary spheres. The beds within the parterre are filled with flowers, such as pink Silene pendula, that bloom in delicious colors. Climbing roses, jasmine, and wisteria curtain the walls creating a luscious backdrop.

The villa itself, a rather simple structure that has grown in size through the ages, has a tower that extends three floors above the roof of the main part of the villa. The tower not only gives the house a grand view of the surrounding countryside and the city below, but also adds architectural character to the building.

Records show that the property was bought by Gino di Lodovico Capponi in 1572, and continued in family hands for some time. In his book, *Great Houses of Italy*, Harold Acton wrote: "The two loggias, one on the southern terrace, another on the northern side, were added in 1882 by Lady Scott, a daughter of the Duke of Portland, and are most convenient in summer when dinner may be served in one and tea in the other. Their pietra serena columns were salvaged from the old market place, demolished to make way for the present Piazza della Repubblica. No doubt it was Lady Scott who planted the smooth lawn running behind the house like the bowling alley at Villa Gamberaia."

Lady Scott's embellishment of the villa and the garden was respectfully added to by the new owners, Mr. and Mrs. Henry Clifford of Philadelphia, who bought the residence in 1928. During the Cliffords' tenure many well-known Europeans and Americans, Adlai Stevenson for one, enjoyed the beauty and tranquility of this well-placed villa. In the care of their present owners, the Aureliano Benedetti family, the gardens are romantic and glorify the Florentine hills.

VILLA L'OMBRELLINO

a garden view that inspires artists and writers

L'Ombrellino, a villa high in the hills of Bellosguardo, does indeed have the "beautiful view" promised by the name of its location. This handsome structure, recently restored as a conference center, dates from 1372. It was the seat of the Segni family for some four hundred years, and was known as Villa di Bellosguardo. In 1617, Lorenzo Segni, the grandson of the historian Bernardo Segni, rented the villa to Galileo. Here, Galileo began to write the historic papers outlining his theory of the movement of the earth and planets. In the early nineteenth century the Ciseri family acquired the villa, and in 1812 the poet Ugo Foscolo, while a guest of the family, began to compose his famous poem, *Le Grazie*. The villa became the property of Contessa Teresa Spinelli in 1815, and it was she who placed a decorative metal umbrella in the garden, which gave the villa its present name, L'Ombrellino.

George and Alice Keppel bought L'Ombrellino in 1925. Mrs. Keppel had been an intimate friend of Edward VII. After his death in 1910 and the havoc of World War I, the Keppels decided they preferred the sun of Italy, and the setting of this spectacular villa and its spacious garden, to life in England. In *The Late Edwardians*, published by the Boston Athenaeum in conjunction with an exhibition, Peter Quennell, a friend of Alice Keppel, made this comment: "During her later life, she exchanged her London house for an ancient villa high above Florence, where she entertained the Tuscan *grand monde*, and everyday, as Osbert Sitwell liked to relate, would walk with her gardener about its flowery terrace, exclaiming 'bisogna begonia'—her knowledge of Italian was rather limited—if she decided that a flowerbed needed some additional embellishment."

Alice and George Keppel died in 1947, within two months of each other, and are buried in the Protestant cemetery, Gli Allori. For the next twenty-five years their daughter, Violet Trefusis, divided her time between L'Ombrellino, Paris, and St. Loup, where she summered. Trefusis was the author

The garden at L'Ombrellino, with its tall cypresses and expanse of green lawn, is a garden for promenades and fêtes.

Overleaf: *A late eighteenth-century engraving by Guesdon shows the great vantage point of the property. The villa's name, L'Ombrellino, comes from the metal umbrella, depicted in the drawing, which was added to the garden in the early nineteenth century by former owner Contessa Teresa Spinelli.*

of a number of books and essays, and some of her voluminous correspondence with friends such as Vita Sackville West, Colette, and François Mitterand have been published. She tells of a privileged, sometimes glittering life, and of a certain social structure, enlivened by artists and writers, that seems to fascinate when viewed from a distance.

Trefusis's friend, Peter Quennell, considered her a myth-maker, and said: "Violet was apt to unfold her legends with a glorious lack of caution." In any case, Violet did strive to retain the elegance of the villa, the grandeur of the garden, and an almost magical life there in memory of her mother.

In *The Late Edwardians*, John Phillips wrote: "The view from L'Ombrellino is dramatic. From the spacious garden terrace, landscaped by Alice Keppel and guarded by a group of baroque statues, one looked over a wall purple with wisteria vines to the vista of Florence beyond." He continues with a quote from Tefusis's book, *Prelude to Misadventures:* "The dome of the Cathedral, the Battistero, the predatory, hawklike silhouette of the Palazzo Vecchio, the sprawled beautifully composed town, which hung back from the Arno's nonchalant escape into the greenest of pastoral landscapes. Everywhere, the punctuation of cypresses, with here and there a stab of purple bougainvillea, gave the right value to church and campanile."

Phillips continued: "The gardens were lovely. There was an ever-changing variety of flowers. Great terra-cotta tubs contained azalea and gardenia plants nurtured in the villa's hothouses. In late spring there was an exuberance of wisteria, honeysuckle, and purple bougainvillea. Violet's special pride was the iris garden with many blossoms of delicate hues. . . . On fine days it was a delight to lunch on the front terrace amid the gardenias and azaleas, or alternately on the more intimate terrace on the other side of the villa, guarded by eighteenth-century stone blackamoors. Violet always picked a gardenia, a boutonniere for each gentleman present, a characteristic gesture."

Opposite: *The baroque figures that stand on the wall contribute to the intoxicating mood of the setting.*

TORRE DI BELLOSGUARDO
a traditional garden surrounding a Tuscan tower

La Torre di Bellosguardo, now run as a luxury hotel, was acquired by the Franchetti family at the end of the last century, and remains in family hands. Barone Amerigo Franchetti has directed the recent restoration of the villa and its garden set on one of the most arresting promontories in the hills of Bellosguardo. The fourteenth-century tower was built as a hunting tower for the Florentine nobleman Guido Cavalcanti, a friend of the political activist and poet Dante. Two centuries later the architect Michelozzo began construction of the house. The Medici confiscated it in 1512.

The renewal of the villa has enhanced the old frescoed walls and rosette-studded ceilings. An update of the garden has infused it with vines, shrubs, and flowering plants which give great color and a sense of *luxe*. As the season begins the garden blooms with lilac, roses, magnolias, wisteria, mimosa, daffodils, camellias, peonies, oleander, cineraria, and blue bugloss. Terraces are encircled with tall umbrella pines and veteran cypresses. One of its greatest features is a long green lawn, prized in traditional Italian garden design. At the end of the lawn, the crowning feature of this villa's garden is the most extraordinary arbor of pale pink roses that spill by the hundreds over an ascending stone stair.

In *The Four Continents*, Osbert Sitwell wrote about the towers of the region: "The towers of northern Italy in general, and of Tuscany in particular, possess a beauty of their own, different from that of towers in the south. They are taller, simpler in line, but larger at the top, bursting into open platforms under pointed arches, as the stalk of a flower burst into blossom. . . . Indeed they have some resemblance in shape to the Florence lily. . . . My Italian home, Montegufoni, stands at the very centre of this country of towers, and from time to time I climb up the steep stairs of my own tower there, in the morning or at night, to allow the feeling of the country round to permeate my consciousness."

The terraces of the garden at Torre di Bellosguardo take advantage of the descending terrain. This terrace is particularly lush and colorful, with beds of brilliantly colored cineraria and blue bugloss. Potted lemon trees run the length of a walkway bordered by clipped boxwood.

Overleaf: A lower garden is centered with a grassy lawn, bordered with cypress, beds of iris, and a vine-covered wall. An umbrella pine helps to shade a stair covered by a most luxuriant rose arbor.

VILLA LA LIMONAIA
a flower-filled garden, a haven for painters

La Limonaia, a villa with extensive grounds high in the hills of Bellosguardo, is known for its large and colorful garden. It takes its name from the boxwood parterre near the house that is splendid with potted lemon trees, spectacular roses, and other plants, such as cineraria and jasmine, that add brilliant color.

Overleaf: *A view of the parterre where floribunda roses and trained climbers thrive.*

Second overleaf: *One of the garden walls is home to an ancient white wisteria with especially long flower clusters. Pine, cypress, and pink rhododendron are also part of the setting.*

Third overleaf: *There are grassy pathways through the field of irises so visitors may enjoy the extravagant flowering.*

Fourth overleaf: *In a lushly green part of the garden, a rose arbor, and pots of pansies lead one toward the iris field below.*

There always seems to be an artist painting in the garden at Villa La Limonaia. From near and far they arrive to be inspired by the fields of flowers and the splendid view of the city of Florence. Brunelleschi's beautiful cathedral dome and other city landmarks give Florence its poetic texture when seen from the hills of Bellosguardo.

In a most advantageous situation, just as the hills begin to ease into a more gentle slope leading to the floor of the Arno valley, the gardens at La Limonaia are open and spacious. The owner, Mrs. Patricia Volterra, sees to it that the slopes, studded with olive, peach, and pear trees, are covered with flowering color through the growing seasons. In the month of May there are fields of iris in many colors, with paths bordered by irises and the small Chinese roses that do so well in and around Florence. The flower symbol of the city is called a lily although it looks like an iris. At La Limonaia, the iris reigns supreme.

The villa, which dates from about 1470, was rebuilt after World War II under the direction of architect Piero Berardi and has since been a setting for gala gatherings of musicians, art dealers, and scholars. Guests often spill out into the parterre garden directly in back of the villa. Reception rooms on the main floor offer a view of and easy access to one of the most colorful gardens in the vicinity. The villa garden is tended by three part-time gardeners, representing three generations of the same family. Roses in particular seem to respond enthusiastically to their touch—roses in all forms—in bushes, trained on trellises, climbing walls, covering arbors, and in the palest to the most brilliant colors. Other things that thrive there: jasmine, cineraria, hortensia, rhododendron, paulownia, and linden trees. It is apparent that the gardeners at La Limonaia have the magical touch that has made Italian plantsmen famous.

BIBLIOGRAPHY

ACTON, HAROLD. *Great Houses of Italy: The Tuscan Villas*. New York: The Viking Press, 1973.

_____. *Memoirs of an Aesthete*. London: Methuen & Co., 1948.

_____. *More Memoirs of an Aesthete*. London: Methuen & Co., 1970.

_____. *The Pazzi Conspiracy*. London: Thames & Hudson, 1979.

_____. *The Villas of Tuscany*. London: Thames & Hudson, 1985.

ACTON, HAROLD, with Edward Chaney. *Florence, A Travellers' Companion*. London: Constable, 1986.

AGNELLI, MARELLA. *Gardens of the Italian Villas*. New York: Rizzoli International Publications, 1987.

ANDERSON, CHARLES R. *Person, Place and Thing in Henry James' Novels*. Durham, NC: Duke University Press, 1977.

ARTOM-TREVES, GUILIANA. *The Golden Ring—The anglo-florentines 1947-1862*. London: Longmans & Co., 1956.

BEATON, CECIL. *The Face of the World: An International Scrapbook of People and Places*. London: Weidenfeld and Nicholson, 1957.

BERENSON, BERNARD. *Sketches for a Self-Portrait*. New York: Pantheon, 1949.

BERTI, LUCIANO. *Florence, the city and its art* Florence: Scala, Instituto Fotografico Editorale, 1979.

CASTELLI, MARCELLA. *I Chiostri di Firenze, entro le mura*. Florence: Becocci Editore, 1982.

CHATFIELD, JUDITH. *A Tour of Italian Gardens*. New York: Rizzoli International Publications, 1988.

CLARKE, ETHNE, and Raffaello Bencini. *The Gardens of Tuscany*. New York: Rizzoli International Publications, 1990.

CRAWFORD, WILLIAM SHARMAN. *Life in Tuscany*. London: Smith, Elder & Co., 1859.

GINORI LISCI, LEONARDO. *The Palazzi of Florence, their history and art*. Florence: Cassa di Risparmio di Firenze, 1985.

GRAHAME, GEORGINA. *In a Tuscan Garden*. London: John Lane, The Bodley Head, 1902.

HAMILTON, OLIVE. *Paradise of Exiles: Tuscany and the British*. London: Andre Deutsch, 1974.

JACOROSSI, MARCELLO. *Introduction to Florence*. Florence: Bonechi Editore, 1968.

LAZZARO, CLAUDIA. *The Italian Renaissance Garden*. New Haven: Yale University Press, 1990.

MASSON, GEORGINA. *Italian Gardens*. London: Thames & Hudson, 1961.

ORIGO, IRIS. *Images and Shadows*. London: John Murray, 1970.

ORLANDI, GIULIO LENSI. *Le Ville di Firenze di là d'Arno*. Florence: Vallecchi Editore, 1954.

OUIDA. *Pascarèl*. London: Chapman and Hall, 1873.

ROSS, JANET. *Florentine Places and their stories*. London: J.M. Dent, 1905.

RUSKIN, JOHN. *Mornings in Florence*. London: George Allen, 1875.

VASARI, GIORGIO. *Lives of the Artists*. New York: Penguin Books, 1987.

WHARTON, EDITH. *Italian Villas and their Gardens*. London: John Lane, The Bodley Head, 1904.

_____. *A Backward Glance*. London: Constable, 1972.

INDEX

The photograph on page 59 appears courtesy of Scala/Art Resource, NY.

Overleaf: *View of Florence from the garden at Villa Capponi.*

Second overleaf: *View of the dome of Santa Maria del Fiore from the loggetta of Palazzo Gondi.*